RELEASED

1929

The Supervisor: Agent for Change in Teaching

Papers from

The ASCD Eleventh Curriculum Research Institute
Washington, D. C., November 6-9, 1965
Denver, Colorado, April 23-26, 1966

•

Edited by
James Raths, Chairman
ASCD Research Commission

and

Robert R. Leeper, Editor
ASCD Publications

Association for Supervision and Curriculum Development, NEA
1201 Sixteenth Street, N.W., Washington, D.C. 20036

Library of Congress Catalog Card Number: 66-29046

Contents

Foreword

GREAT institutions are notoriously slow to change and education is no exception. The lag between the best we know and its implementation in practice is a continual problem for curriculum workers. The reduction of this lag is especially important in times like these when the rate of change in the world has so vastly accelerated and when the entire nation has turned its face to education for the solution of some of its most pressing problems.

A major objective of the Association for Supervision and Curriculum Development has long been to facilitate the movement of ideas from their formulation in theory and research into practice in the public schools. One of the ways it does this is through the programs of its research institutes. In these we have sought to bring together scholars from the learned disciplines with educators in key positions to innovate change in education.

In addition, the papers of many of these research institutes have been made available to a wider audience through ASCD publications. The titles of some of these former reports are as follows: *Language and Meaning; Theories of Instruction; Intellectual Development: Another Look; Nurturing Individual Potential; New Dimensions in Learning; Human Variability and Learning; Freeing Capacity To Learn* and *Learning More About Learning.*

The papers in this publication, as James Raths indicates in his preface, are particularly concerned with modern thinking and research in supervision. As a distinct profession, supervision is a comparative newcomer among educational occupations but a rapidly growing one. This profession is especially important in these times, for supervisors are change agents in the schools. The major task of supervision is the facilitation of growth and development in teachers and pupils. It has the crucial task of feeding into the bloodstream of education the best information and practices available. Until fairly recently there has been little research upon which the supervisor could draw for guidance in defining his proper roles and functions. This picture is changing, however, and the papers presented in these research institutes represent but a few of the research efforts we can expect to see in the years just ahead.

ASCD is indebted to Dr. Raths and to his research commission for the work they have done in making these curriculum research institutes possible. We believe they have made a valuable contribution toward the advancement of the profession. It is our hope that the publication of these papers may provide increased understanding and help for supervisors in practice and may stimulate further research in this area of great need.

November 1966   ARTHUR W. COMBS, *President*
                                          Association for Supervision
                                          and Curriculum Development

Preface

THE Eleventh Curriculum Research Institute of the Association for Supervision and Curriculum Development was intended to shed some light on research in supervision. We have assumed for some time that supervisors are needed and that without them, schools would be less effective. What do the data say? As we planned the Institute, the members of the ASCD Research Commission became aware that there was very little research in this area—with the exception of perception studies which seemed to show that the supervisor's role is not perceived by teachers, or by principals, as it is perceived by the supervisors themselves. However, we were fortunate in finding eight scholars who agreed to share with us their research and their views concerning supervision.

First, James B. Macdonald placed concerns of supervision into several contexts—each suggesting a dilemma that poses far-reaching philosophical and ethical questions. It is safe to say that none of the papers which followed were able to meet the arguments implicit in Macdonald's contribution. Yet this is not to suggest that the papers were not germane to the topic, but rather that data are perhaps improper sources for answers to philosophical questions. Macdonald's contribution remained, however, as an intellectual setting within which the various papers which followed inevitably were seen.

Boyd and Ringness presented papers about five months and 2000 miles apart (the former gave his paper at Washington, D. C., in November while the latter read his contribution for the Western Section of the Institute in April at Denver, Colorado), but they were very similar in content. These two scholars are concerned with the psychological mechanisms that are operating between the teacher and the supervisor. They seem to hold that if supervisors could find out more about the drives, motives and problems of teachers, the process of supervision would be greatly enhanced.

Amidon and Powell, and Ward gave papers reporting on the efficacy of various feedback procedures. While Amidon and Powell's feedback system deals only with information concerning interaction patterns, Ward's project was wider in scope and also was planned to enhance communication between the researcher on the one hand and the teacher on the other. These studies suggest that supervisors may indeed profitably spend their time providing feedback to teachers under certain conditions. In this role, a supervisor may do less interpreting, as would a supervisor following the ideas of Boyd and Ringness, but he would do more describing of what he is seeing.

The papers of Harris and Bishop are less empirical and more prescriptive in nature. They identify problems in the area of supervision and suggest ways in which the problems can be met. Harris' suggestions are mostly for the scholar and his study of supervision. Bishop, by way of contrast, suggests actions that individual supervisors can take at this critical time in education.

In the final paper of this booklet, March relates the findings of several organizational researches. Seen as a member of an organization, the supervisor needs to understand how an organization functions. March presents several models, not any of them totally acceptable, for examining the functioning of an organization. He draws implications for supervision and for supervisors as a result of his work in non-educational field research. His contributions suggest that many of us need to examine some of our basic assumptions regarding the importance of consistency and coordination within an organization.

The Research Commission and the Association for Supervision and Curriculum Development would like to extend appreciation to the staff members of the two sections of this Institute who helped make the experiences more meaningful. The names of these very able persons follow: *Eastern Section*—Margaret Ammons, University of Wisconsin, Madison; Edwina Deans, U.S. Office of Education; Marie DeCarlo, Public Schools, Montgomery County, Maryland; Benjamin Ebersole then of the Association staff and now with the Public Schools, Baltimore County, Maryland; Jack W. Miller, George Peabody College for Teachers; Audrey Norris, Public Schools, Willoughby, Ohio; Hugh Perkins, University of Maryland; and Theodore Storlie, Public Schools, Flossmoor, Illinois; *Western Section*—Charles Galloway, North Texas State University; Inabell Kirby, Public Schools, Decatur, Illinois; James Popham, University of California, Los Angeles; and Bernard Spodek, University of Illinois; *both Sections*—Louise M. Berman of the Association staff; Eli Bower, National Institute of Mental Health; and James B. Macdonald then of the University of Wisconsin, Madison and now with the University of Wisconsin-Milwaukee.

Also, the Association for Supervision and Curriculum Development would like to acknowledge its indebtedness to the National Institute of Mental Health for co-sponsoring the Eleventh Curriculum Research Institute.

August 1966   JAMES RATHS, *Chairman*
ASCD Research Commission

Acknowledgments

Final editing of the manuscript and production of this booklet were the responsibility of Robert R. Leeper, Associate Secretary and Editor, ASCD Publications. Technical production was handled by Mary Ann Lurch, Editorial Assistant, assisted by Teola T. Jones, Staff Assistant, under the general supervision of Ruth P. Ely, Editorial Associate.

Helping Teachers Change

James B. Macdonald

SUPERVISION has traditionally been thought of in terms of an economic decision-making model. Both government and industry have espoused and utilized this model within their own unique contexts.

In educational terms, this model suggests that the function of a supervisor is primarily to monitor and to work with teachers toward the more effective and efficient achievement of the goals of the school. The goals of the school have most often been defined in terms of children's learning. Variations in this model have occurred with the influence of the progressive education movement, group dynamics psychology, and mental health concepts. Model variations due to these influences, in essence, shifted the goals of supervisors from the student to the teacher. The teacher was characterized as an individual with his own needs, interests and aspirations which must be accounted for in the supervisory process. Further, group dynamics studies seemed to indicate that in order to help the individual teacher certain dynamic processes of communication and interaction were necessary components.

In recent years, with the decline of public support for "Progressive" education, the shift in supervisory focus within the individual teacher-centered ideology has been attached to the public's growing concern for mental health, with the result that some models of supervision are semi-therapeutic in structure.

It appears now that we are entering yet another era in supervision, the era of feedback. This era is difficult to dignify with the term scientific, yet its major emphasis is upon the "objective" provision of information to teachers about their practices. Major efforts today are being made in the development of descriptive models of teaching that may be used as "mirrors" to be held up by supervisors for teachers to see their own behavior. In essence this is a move to utilize research tools for in-service education functions.

1

In historical perspective, the various models of supervision alluded to here leave open a major question: "What, if anything, does supervisory activity, regardless of model, contribute to education?"

We act essentially upon faith that supervision is effective. This faith arises from our experiencing of supervision and not essentially from research data sources. Rather, our faith projects a rationale that says:

Some teachers are continually changing—growing toward better teaching. They seem to be able to find a way to develop almost "in spite of" their environments. No matter how rigid the school policies are or how static the administration may be, such teachers seem to prosper. Perhaps these teachers are the creative ones, and/or probably this behavior is an integral part of their personality. We recognize this type of person and we bemoan the fact that there are too few teachers like this.

If all teachers could grow in this way there might be no need for in-service programs. The reality of the situation is that the majority of our teachers do not display a noticeable built-in professional-growth mechanism. Like the population at large, there seem to be relatively few self-educating people in teaching.

Most teachers are in fact caught up in the "organization," the educational bureaucracy. The problems of status and role in the system, their relationships to principals, other teachers, parents, and central administrators are pressing and pressuring. School curricula, policies, procedures, mores and customs become the base for working with youngsters rather than a facilitating milieu surrounding the basic problems of teaching the young. It is little wonder that few of our teachers can overcome the burden of the "system" and become self-educating.

Apparently it is necessary and desirable that we find ways to stimulate and guide the professional growth of most teachers. This, one must suppose, is the central rationale for all productive in-service programs.

The Value Dilemma

Setting out to change teacher behavior, however, is a specific instance of the broader problem in our society of the manipulation of human behavior. The moral issue here is the very same issue involved in Chinese Communist "brainwashing," or the development of some Utopia by the utilization of operant conditioning, or the shaping of cultural taste by the advertising industry.

We have unsuccessfully tried to avoid this issue by the acceptance of the following pattern of reasoning: Teacher actions x, y, and z are the most efficient ways of achieving goals 1, 2, and 3. Efficiency in the achievement of goals produces a greater profit in the learning outcomes of children. The "profit" of increased learning outcomes is the central criterion of the worth of actions x, y, and z. Therefore, all teachers should perform these actions. Most of our research in teacher effectiveness embodies this format.

This neat logical pattern has at least three serious drawbacks in its reasoning. First, we have little, if any, knowledge of predictable chains of behavior that can be given all teachers in the form, x, y, and z, with the guarantee that 1, 2, and 3 will result. Thus, we do not know what specific teacher actions will produce specific desired results. Beyond this we do not agree that "profit" in the form of learning outcomes is the only criterion of worth, and a third drawback relates to our confusion about how the learning of new behavior takes place. Thus, we are not sure what actions will result in what; nor whether we have a right to demand these behaviors if we know them; or even how to develop these behaviors if we can eliminate the above considerations. These dilemmas can be called the *empirical*, the *moral*, and the *theoretical dilemmas*.

Thus, empirically, we have yet to specify the chains from teacher behavior to pupil learning. Morally, we face the dilemma of deciding whether we should approach the changing of teacher behavior with some criterion which lies outside the person of the teacher (e.g., pupil learning) as a basis for change, and, theoretically we do not agree upon how to proceed with the business of changing behavior.

These dilemmas, at this time, can only be resolved by some statement of premises or propositions upon which an in-service program can be built. This writer believes the following premises are justified:

1. Teaching is a complex integration of behaviors and single behavior chains cannot profitably be grafted onto the teacher's behavioral system.

2. It is morally wrong to set out to change teacher behavior unless the change sought has been rationally selected by the teacher from among a range of known alternatives.

3. Learning is an individual matter and how something is learned is determined primarily by the internal structure of needs, perceptions, readiness, motivations, etc., of the individual—not by the external conditions of an outside person desiring change.

Conditions for Professional Growth

Accepting the basic premise just stated, there seem to be at least four sets of conditions that are acceptable and desirable for the stimulation and guidance of the change in teacher behavior.

Social Setting for Change

We are prone to the exclusive use of psychological or sociopsychological metaphors when talking about change. Change becomes synonymous with personality change, or new individual learning. We have laid aside a basic fact of social existence, the effect of the social system upon individual behavior. This is highly unfortunate, for interpersonal interaction and other conditions for growth are highly dependent upon political, economic and administrative confirmation for their effectiveness.

Teacher growth must not be a game to be played by teachers in order to gain status and roles, financial reward, or professional recognition within the right boundaries. The boundaries of the system must be flexible and the system must function as if the phenomena of teacher change are natural and desirable.

Economically, the school system should provide ample funds for fostering growth by making available money to accomplish change. This not only consists of the usual concept of research and development funds, but also includes availability of funds for the personal growth of teachers. No stronger setting could be created than the "natural" provision and "expectation" of use of funds for these purposes.

The politics of the school system are also a crucial consideration. It is the inner workings of the power structure that often are either covert or overt handicaps for development. The allocation of rewards must be focused upon the goals of schools and consequently the growth of teachers rather than the service to the system.

A highly centralized power structure defeats this goal. Further, when access to power is not available to those with talent and a willingness to accept the inherent responsibility that accrues, then the goals of the school are seen as a front for the real purpose—the giving and maintaining of status and role situations. Thus, schools should be organized in small units where access to power (if need be, administration) is earned and is accessible to all qualified from time to time. Under these circumstances the central purpose of the schools, the education of the young, may be in central focus and allied with the growth of teachers.

Administrative practices may sometimes reflect and sometimes at least partially determine economic and political forces. From a teacher's viewpoint, school policy is witnessed through the agency of administrators. The role of administrators in relation to teachers is clearly implied in the last three conditions. It is only important here to remind ourselves that the administrator symbolizes the setting and is the focal point for teacher observation and perception of the system.

An Interpersonal Climate for Change

An interpersonal climate which encourages change can arise when the threats of failure, condemnation and negative judgment are removed and a challenging and stimulating environment is constructed.

A challenging environment for teachers is one in which new ideas, materials, practices, programs and other innovations are brought to their awareness, discussed and made available for the curious and daring to try. In other words, if teachers are going to change they must see new alternatives to the practices they now use. These alternatives can be supplied by the school leadership personnel in the form of stimulation through planning for and guiding teachers toward awareness of new alternatives. The use of consultants, speakers, workshops, curriculum meetings, staff displays, materials centers, and professional meetings are a few of the means by which this can be accomplished. It should be noted that the knowledge about and enthusiasm for new practices on the part of the leadership personnel are probably the single greatest factors in the environment.

Teachers, as people, will rarely change without another concomitant aspect in this environment. Threat must be removed so that teachers will take risks. The threat of peer and/or staff disapproval for attempting something new, the threat of evaluation, judgment of worth (merit, etc.) and/or the threat of the unknown results are all operative in teaching.

To lessen threat and encourage the taking of risks by trying out new behaviors, demands, as Rogers [1] says, a strong element of support and positive regard in the surrounding climate. Teachers must feel that other staff and leadership personnel are supportive and regard them as worthwhile persons no matter what they try or do not try.

This climate of lessened threat can be fostered by making most curriculum activities voluntary (it is as important to preserve the right *not* to change as to change) and by striving diligently in all contacts with staff members to demonstrate clearly the fact that you are with and behind them, and that you regard them as worthwhile and productive people. It goes without saying that these feelings must be authentic, not artificial.

A climate for change may well not be enough. Most teachers, like other people, do not have a close and realistic view of their own behavior. They are not close to the reality of their teaching actions. Thus, many

[1] Carl R. Rogers. *On Becoming A Person*. Boston: Houghton Mifflin Company. 1961.

teachers do not actually know what their present teaching behavior is like. There is a need for some process by which a teacher receives a feedback other than his own perceptions of the behavior of his students.

Provision of Reality Testing Procedures

It is imperative that the concept of reality-testing or feedback be clarified. At one time this meant the judgment of the principal or supervisor. It should be pointed out that this is not only irrelevant but detrimental to the testing of reality. The values of principals and supervisors are no doubt real, but they are not the kind of feedback that will best facilitate change. What is needed is some means of helping the teacher see what he is actually doing.

A number of such procedures have been developed during the past decade. Two illustrations may suffice to prove a clarification of this idea. Amidon and Flanders [2] have presented an interaction analysis procedure which provides a picture of teacher behavior to the teacher. As Amidon and Flanders say:

Programs organized for helping teachers to understand their behavior and to plan behavior change must have *provision for an effective feedback system*.[3]

The Flanders system analyzes verbal behavior in the classroom. An outline of the categories follows:

Teacher Talk	*Student Talk*
Indirect	8. Response to teacher
1. Accepts feeling	9. Initiates discussion
2. Praises or encourages	10. Silent or confused.[4]
3. Accepts or uses idea of student	
4. Asks questions	
Direct	
5. Lectures	
6. Gives direction	
7. Criticizes students or	
justifies authority	

An observer sits in the classroom and every three seconds writes down the category number of the interaction he is observing. Over a 40 minute period of time, e.g., with about 20 numbers a minute, an inter-

[2] Edmund J. Amidon and Ned A. Flanders. *The Role of the Teacher in the Classroom: A Manual for Understanding and Improving Teachers' Classroom Behavior.* Minneapolis, Minnesota: Paul S. Amidon & Associates, Inc., 1963.

[3] *Ibid.*, p. 4.

[4] *Ibid.*, p. 6.

action matrix can be built which describes behavior over this period of time.[5]

The important point is that the teacher now has an objective basis or feedback of behavior in the classroom upon which to base a decision to change. He may like what he sees, or he may want to try to modify certain aspects of the situation.

Another feedback approach is the use of learning episodes. Lund and Herrick[6] have been developing this procedure for a number of years. Class sessions are taped and transcribed. The teacher sits down with a transcription and the recording and listens to the playback, following and noting on the transcriptions any relevant comments. Discussion with the supervisor or consultant helps clarify what has happened and the teacher then plans to try out some new approach or behavior if he sees this as desirable. Teachers construct their own categories for analysis of their behavior. This approach is more flexible and less exact than Flanders' analysis. It is somewhat more practical. Variations of this approach are possible by using the episodes for general analysis by other teachers as well as the specific teacher from whom the record was collected. The important aspect of the use of learning episodes, as is the case with interaction analysis, is the provision of some form of objective feedback to the teacher.

Results of these types of feedback procedures would certainly indicate the desirability of school leadership personnel developing and utilizing some system of feedback with teachers that is not used as an evaluation system by evaluators, but as a feedback system by facilitators of change.

The Clarification Process

Most of us would agree that until we know the facts we are not entitled to an opinion. The feedback process described above provides us with the facts, in a stimulating and supportive climate. Change should be forthcoming under these conditions. However, there is still a concern for the direction of the change.

It should be clear from the basic premise stated earlier and the processes already described that the direction for change, the value element in change, must come from the teacher and not be imposed by leadership personnel. Nevertheless, this does not mean that concern for values

---

[5] See, *op. cit.* for further details.

[6] Grace Lund and Virgil E. Herrick. "Using Learning Episodes in Teacher Education." Unpublished manuscript. School of Education, University of Wisconsin, Madison.

is abdicated by school officials. On the contrary, the concern for values is in essence more imperative, though in a different way than before.

Providing teachers with alternatives and choices based on the feedback knowledge of their own teaching behavior does not insure automatically that teachers will make reasonable and desirable decisions (from *their* point of view) without a further condition—the systematic clarification of values and stimulation of thinking by teachers.

Louis Raths[7] has elaborated this process clearly in relation to a teacher's work with children. This process would appear to have just as much merit for school leadership personnel working with staff.

Teachers are exposed to many conflicting patterns of teaching behavior. They have experienced the work of many teachers themselves; they have been encouraged to behave in certain ways in teacher education programs; and they, too, experience the pressures of parents, school policies, peer groups and leadership personnel. These various forces do not provide an integrated common value pattern. On the contrary, there are wide divergencies within this total perspective. Under these conditions it is quite doubtful that teachers possess a highly integrated professional value system of their own. Rather, it is the responsibility of principals, supervisors and other leaders to help teachers to develop their values. One way to do this is by using the clarification process.

Signs exhibited by teachers with value problems may be observed on all staffs. Some of the behaviors which can indicate this are:

1. *Dull, apathetic teaching:* Teachers who are not directed by accepted values may gradually grow apathetic and listless in their teaching behavior.

2. *Highly structured traditionalists:* Lacking values of their own, these teachers have grabbed the traditional system and structured their behavior to conform to it. The direction of their behavior comes from outside themselves in the process of gaining the security of another's available value system.

3. *Perennial dissenters:* There are those teachers who dissent continuously. They disagree with everyone and everything. They never propose a value but they always are against the values of others. They are "rebels without a cause." They are dissenting from the imposition of others' values upon them, but they lack values of their own.

4. *Hesitant and uncertain teachers:* Some teachers never seem to

[7] Louis Raths. "Sociological Knowledge and Needed Curriculum Research." *Research Frontiers in the Study of Children's Learning.* Madison: School of Education, University of Wisconsin.

act with decision and precision. They are forever torn between this and that, uncertain as to which direction to go and hesitant when they tentatively commit themselves. It would seem that these teachers need value development.

5. *Role players in teaching:* Not too occasionally one sees the teacher who bases his teaching behavior principally on a role, a pose, so to speak. He may be the buddy-type, or the humorous type, or the strict type. Whatever his pose, it represents the security of a role-pose instead of the development of a sound internal value system.

6. *Highly inconsistent teachers:* On again, off again, high and low, these teachers show wide fluctuations in teaching behavior; moving from one extreme to another. What values do they have to guide them?

These behavior patterns and others may indicate the need for professional values to guide teacher change, and when they do, then the clarification process is an important way to help this value growth.

The clarification process is focused upon eliciting the expression of the professional and personal beliefs, feelings, attitudes, interests, purposes and aspirations of teachers. When these are expressed, the principal or supervisor listens and the subsequent questioning attempts to focus upon values involved. Any number of questions may be relevant, but the essential of each is that they focus the teacher inward, and there are questions that can only be answered by the teacher. Thus, there is no standard answer (the question is not rhetorical) that can be judged for adequacy. A clarifying question involves a non-judgmental procedure.

You can repeat back what the teacher has said for him to hear; or you can ask "is this what you mean?" or "what are your definitions of terms?" You might ask the teacher to tell more about this idea, or comment that you do not see where this leads, what the consequences are. You might ask whether he believes all teachers should think this way, or ask him for the assumptions underlying the statement.

In all events you attempt to stimulate a thoughtful, clarifying procedure through the expressions of teachers. In the process of this intent you might ask teachers to use the feedback facts to make comparisons of two different occasions, or ask them to summarize a session, or classify their behaviors; to criticize what they see and analyze it; to imagine how they could improve their teaching and to plan for change. You can help them set up their own action research studies. All these approaches provide *ways of thinking with values* or *uses for clarified values.*

In summary, the conditions for teacher change are predicated upon the basic premise of complexity of teaching, integrity of individual teachers, and the integrativeness of the learning process. Given these premises the process of change is best facilitated by:

1. Creating a positive and stimulating social setting for change

2. Developing positive and supporting interpersonal relations

3. Providing reality testing procedures

4. Developing rational thinking and valuing through the clarification process.

This means a loosening of control in the change process which is not only desirable, but which may well be socially realistic (see paper by March, this volume). What it means, in essence, is the rational planning of an environmental milieu within which change operates through a process of freedom and personal choice.

An Interaction Model
Applied to Supervision

Robert D. Boyd

SUPERVISION may be examined within the context of communication. Meanings are given to behaviors. As a supervisor observes and listens, he encodes and decodes what he perceives. In turn, he delivers messages to the supervisee on the bases of his encoding and decoding. The supervisee does likewise within his own frame of reference. Within the supervision situation, messages and interpretation of messages flow and mingle at a tremendous rate in the stream of interaction.

The analogy of a river serves our purposes in illustrating certain problems occurring in supervision as they may be examined within the context of communication. One such problem occurs when either or both the supervisor and supervisee become overly aware of a particular current to the exclusion of the general direction of the river. For example, each sends and receives information about the function of autonomy in teaching-learning situations. This topic is pursued to the exclusion of the fostering of industry, the development of ego identity, and the encouragement of initiative. The narrowness of the direction and content of the messages could not be realized unless the supervisor possessed a knowledge wider than the particular current within the river. The need to have knowledge of the basic structure of the river that is to be navigated should be abundantly obvious.

Both supervisee and supervisor may, at times, get caught up in the eddies of emotional concerns and faulty cognitive structures. The analysis of communication by a knowledgeable supervisor would quickly identify the eddies and whirlpools. With knowledge, some could be avoided and the remainder could be prevented from shipwrecking the whole enterprise. Like a navigator, a supervisor out of the nature of the enterprise has to know where he is going and has to have technical operational knowledge of the means to get there.

Tools—and the Ends Sought

It is essential that this latter point be fully comprehended. A supervisor must have a technical operational knowledge of the means by which to achieve the objectives of the program. There are two aspects to the concept of knowledge as it is employed here. One aspect is understandings; the other is the effective utilization of performance skills in using some set of means. The importance of understandings, although ignored by some psychologists, is assumed here to be basic to a functional education. But understandings do not provide by themselves the power to build. Tools and the skills to use them are the necessary complements to understandings. The progress that man has made rests both upon the understandings that have been developed to explain what men have perceived and imagined and upon tool-making that has extended the reach and power of our own innate feeble tool capacity. Both, in complement, make it possible for us to walk out among the stars.

Educators are and should be among the great tool users. The concept *tool,* as I use the term here, means a conceptual device which, to the extent that the user understands the purposes and structures of the device, and to the extent that he possesses the skills essential to use the device, provides the user a means to analyze or synthesize a set of events unique to the device. Conceptual tools have been categorized as paradigms, models, theories, methods, techniques, etc. In the field of education there are many examples: the taxonomies of objectives, Guilford's three faces of intelligence, Test-Operate-Test-Exit, Developmental Tasks, and others.

To have a conversant level of knowledge about a set of conceptual tools in the areas of curriculum, instruction and learning, is not adequate for qualifying a professional educator. Tools are designed to do work and they can only be put to work effectively and efficiently by those who are skilled in their use. To dismiss the need for the development of skills in the application of conceptual tools on the basis that most tools are crude and inadequate, is analogous to throwing away a flint-stone because it is not a match. It can be readily appreciated that much work needs to be done in improving the tools we have and in producing tools in those areas where there are none. These latter observations are not the issue. Rather, the issue is that the education of educators does not demand and discipline for the intelligent and skillful application, analysis, synthesis and evaluation of conceptual tools employed in the areas of curriculum, instruction and learning.

The educational psychologist is and should be deeply involved with this issue. The function of educational psychology in large part is to develop and test conceptual tools in the areas of human development and adaptation. Tools by which to conceptualize learning, motivation, perception, instruction, communication, etc., are what he seeks in order that he may subsequently be able to explain human behavior in educational situations.

The choice of a set of tools and the ends which are sought through the application of the chosen set of tools are issues in the domain of valuation. The identifying, defining and defending of a valuation system are basic and crucial to intelligent and consistent decision making. If we, as educators, conceive the learner to be passive and receptive, we would select one set of tools. If we conceive the learner to be active and adaptive, we would select another set of tools. Every conceptual tool that educational psychologists invent rests on a set of assumptions about learning, the nature of the human being, and the nature of the human enterprise. The conceptual tool that I am going to describe and discuss has been built on a set of valuation assumptions.

A primary role of the educational psychologist is to work toward the elimination of valuation assumptions in education through accepted procedures of scientific inquiry. In doing their work the educational psychologists have on several occasions developed conceptual tools which greatly aid teachers in carrying out educative processes. In this sense the educational psychologist may be categorized as a toolmaker.

Let us now examine a conceptual tool that should have significant meaning and application in the field of supervision. The utility of any instrument in the final phase rests on the conceptual flexibility and initiative of those who are to use the instrument. Rockets, known to the Chinese for hundreds of years, remained for them simply artifacts of ritual symbolism.

Three Channels of Communication

Here then, is a conceptual tool in a form of a model which uncovers for us the dynamic interdependent variables in communication. I have called it the three-channel system.

As I have observed groups and have listened to and restudied the transcriptions of group interactions, I have become very much aware of two constituents to interaction. One constituent is the symbolic patterns, the other is the content conveyed through the symbolic patterns. Symbolic patterns are gestures and linguistic structures. The raised eyebrow or the shrug of the shoulders are examples of gestures. Examples of linguistic structures are questions, exclamations, assertions. I refer to linguistic structures as utterances.

An utterance may not only be classified by type of linguistic structure but also by content. The term *content* includes more than subject matter or information on a particular subject. Content of an utterance also includes a motivational and a delivery component as well as a subject matter component. I shall attempt in the following sections of this paper to make clear what is meant by the three components. These three components are viewed in their dynamic phase as the three channels of communication. (See Figure 1.)

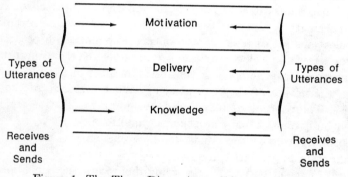

Figure 1. The Three Dimensions of Communication

Motivational Channel

One function of language is in the service of basic concerns. Basic concerns may be conceptualized in any one of a number of motivation and personality theories. The theory of ego crises, for several reasons, appears to be a most productive theoretical framework and it is that theory which is employed in the present study. Thus, the motivational aspect of an utterance is identified according to the particular ego crisis which is being expressed. For example, a question, in an interaction sequence, that is seeking the structuring of authority may be defined as having as its motivational component the ego crisis of autonomy.[1]

An examination of one's own experiences in an interpersonal inter-

[1] It should not be inferred from this sole, isolated analysis that the individual contributing the particular utterance has the crisis of autonomy as a central concern. The only relevant point that can be made at this juncture of the analysis is that the particular utterance is expressing the ego crisis or concern for autonomy as its motivational content.

action sequence may prove to be constructive at this point. As one listens to (and watches) a person talking, he may begin to perceive certain concerns which are being expressed. The concerns may appear openly in the surface flow of his conversation or discussion. The concerns may appear just as frequently in less open vision, coming to the surface with this word or that gesture.

The person may be telling him about his work-a-day experiences and running through his accounts are consistent threads of perceived mistrust of his fellow workers. Such concerns openly displayed or masked behind words and gestures are perceived as the motivational content of the utterance.

Elsewhere (3; 4) the author has presented the reasons and rationale for selecting ego psychology conceptualizations of motivation, specifically in the work of Erik Erikson (5; 6). Briefly, the argument may be presented in the following terms. Basic motivation may be defined as the desire to overcome and the expression of resolving an irritability arising in the physio-psycho-social fields of interaction of an organism. So defined, motivation cannot be studied directly. Only the behavioral manifestations of the inner processes involved in the handling of the irritabilities may be observed and studied. Unfortunately there is no justification to assume that the many facets of the total confrontation between the adaptive forces and agencies and the irritabilities come to the level of observable overt behavior. Clinical evidence has demonstrated that such total observation and even awareness are not readily perceived or obtained.

It is at this point that we must clearly realize the point alluded to earlier that since irritabilities are expressed in physio-psycho-social fields, the meanings that the irritabilities come to have transcend intra-interpretations, and require inter-interpretations between the organism and its environment. Here the concept ego provides the bridge uniting, through "meaning," the inner life of the individual and its dynamic involvements with its environments (7). In brief, our argument is that motivation may be studied by observing the problems the ego is working on and by categorizing these problems into a life-span, physio-psycho-social personality system.

The most elaborate and operational statement of ego development has been given by Erik Erikson in a series of clear and brilliant writings. In these writings, Erikson has presented a new theory of personality development which extends Freud's theory of psychosexual development of the libido into the sphere of ego processes. The ego is seen as a developing part of personality in its own right. Ego development is assumed to take place in a systematic fashion in combination with libido developmental processes and general motivation processes. Erikson divided ego development into eight stages. He postulated that each stage is focal to a certain chronological period of life, and that at each of these periods the ego faces a central problem or crisis. Havighurst (9) has developed a similar rationale under the rubric "developmental tasks."

Figure 2 is an epigenetic diagram of the eight ego crises. The figure is to be read from the top left corner diagonally to the bottom right corner. Each diagonal cell should be connected and read with the corresponding age period which appears at the left margin of the figure. For example, the ego-stage, autonomy vs shame and doubt, is connected to and read with the muscular-anal chronological period.

	1	2	3	4	5	6	7	8
I Oral-Sensory	Trust vs. Mistrust							
II Muscular-Anal		Autonomy vs. Shame Doubt						
III Locomotor-Genital			Initiative vs. Guilt					
IV Latency				Industry vs. Inferiority				
V Puberty and Adolescence					Identity vs. Role Diffusion			
VI Young Adulthood						Intimacy vs. Isolation		
VII Adulthood							Generativity vs. Stagnation	
VIII Maturity								Integrity vs. Disgust Despair

Figure 2. The Eight Stages of Man
(After Erikson, 1950.)

It is beyond the scope of this paper to explain fully Erikson's contributions to the theory of ego-stage development. However, it may be of some help to present a brief explanation of one ego-stage in order that the reader may grasp the nature of the particular conceptual framework.

The first stage, trust vs. mistrust, is identified by Erikson as the "oral-respiratory-sensory stage" (6: 166). This is the physiological aspect in the physio-psycho-social triad that the ego must handle. Erikson goes on to state that trust is established initially by:

... consistency, continuity, and a sameness of experience (which) provide a rudimentary sense of ego identity which depends, I think, on the recognition that there is an inner population of remembered and anticipated sensations and images which are firmly correlated with the outer population of familiar and predictable things and people (5:219).

Here he expresses the psycho-social aspects of ego development.

Having a knowledge at the analysis and synthesis level of this particular conceptual framework should provide a means by which to categorize the motivational aspect of utterances. The examples which follow may illustrate the procedures.

A student teacher speaking to a supervisor may say:

1. "It's a lot of fun to start projects with the children." Here is positive initiative.

2. "Some children don't seem to like me, at least they never seem to want to be openly friendly toward me." Here is the ego crisis of intimacy. One should also be aware of concern in the crisis of basic trust.

3. "Teaching has a lot of satisfaction for me but I still don't know whether it is for me."

The crisis of role identity is foremost in this utterance. It is essential to listen most carefully, for the primary concern may lie elsewhere. There may be concern in crisis of industry or in basic trust. Listening carefully and asking questions should help to reveal where the weight of the problem lies.

Delivery Channel

Another of the three content components of an utterance is delivery. An utterance may be spoken, or delivered in a wide variety of manners. For example, the word "no" may be spoken sternly, questioningly, laughingly, firmly or mildly. One commonly may hear an individual remark: "It is not so much what he says that irritates me, but the way in which he says it." Another similar remark that may be heard during a break session of a group is: "There is something in John's manner that just rubs me the wrong way." Style of delivery has long been a concern of students of speech.

Novelists go to great length to describe their characters in terms of delivery styles and the meanings that are attached to these behaviors.

. . . the Italian's face changed instantly and assumed the look of offensive, affected sweetness, which was evidently its habitual expression in conversation with women.[2]

. . . Sonya gave him an intensely furious look, and, hardly able to restrain her tears, though there was still a constrained smile on her lips, she got up and went out of the room. All Nikolay's animation was gone.[3]

Delivery styles portray meanings. It is the scientist's responsibility to develop a system of categories that does as little violence as possible to the meanings of behavior. The simpler the system of categories the more immediately usable these categories may be. Many researchers have struggled with the problem of categorizing behavior. Among them, the works of Bion and of Thelen with his associates appeared to be ideally suited to the needs of the present research. The material which follows draws heavily on their works.

There are two content aspects in delivery style, work and emotionality. Work aspects of group operations have been defined as, "the consciously determined, deliberate, reality-bound, goal-seeking aspects of the group's activities" (10: 13). There are four types of work (10):

Level 1. This level of work is personally need-oriented.

One-level statements are triggered off by what is happening in the group but they are expressions of personal need and are not group-oriented. Energy is bound up with the internal situation of the individual rather than with the interactive situation (11: 28).

Level 2. This level of work involves setting up the structure within which they may work on the task. Behaviors included in this level may involve attempting to define the task, taking care of the housekeeping needs and details, searching for and clarifying means and plans by which to achieve the completion of the task.

Level 3. This level of work is ". . . group-focused work which usually has some new ingredient. It tends to be recognizable as active problem solving" (11: 29).

Behaviors included in this category are: indications of thought-in-process leading to understanding, introspection, reasoning, reckoning, musing, cogitating, spelling out relations, cause and effect, exploring, testing, categorizing, etc.

Level 4. This level of work is creative, insightful and interpretive.

[2] Leo Tolstoy. *War and Peace.*
[3] *Ibid.*

Four-level work usually involves an appropriate (i.e., the group is ready for it) and insightful interpretation which brings together for the group a whole series of experiences and infuses meaning into them, and at the same time has immediate relevance to present problems (11: 29).

The emotionality aspects of group operation have been defined as ". . . non-purposive, 'instinctual,' and not under conscious control" (10: 13). There are six types of emotionalities or emotional states:[4]

Fight statements express hostility and aggression. Behaviors included within this category are: attacking, rebuking, punishing, blocking, dividing (the group), warning, threatening, expressing hostile resistance, self-aggrandizing (at the expense of others), scapegoating, ridiculing, criticizing, opposing, disagreeing, rejecting, disapproving, etc.

Flight statements express avoidance and withdrawal. Behaviors included within this category are: making or engaging in light humor, over-intellectualizing, dealing with trivia, giving off-the-point comments, overgeneralizing, manifesting impatience (to leave and move on), unattending, mumbling, non-responding, etc.

Pairing statements express warmth, intimacy and supportiveness. Behaviors included in this category are: friendliness, unusual responsiveness, side remarks to another, expressions of commendation, enthusiasm to a member or to the group as a whole, demonstrations of affection, love and sexuality, encouraging others, rewarding, approving, reassuring, bolstering, admiring, adoring, sharing, supplying, showing compassion and tenderness, mediating, conciliating, moderating, cooperating, etc.

Counter-pairing statements express desire for formality, aloofness, noninvolvement on the interpersonal level. Behaviors included in this category are: seeking or maintaining interpersonal detachment, resistance to casualness in groups, non-affectionate, formal, withholding love or friendship, impassive, rigid and cool in friendship situations, unapproachable, impersonal, distant, reserved, works against friendship groups (on the basis that this destroys the group as a whole), etc.

Dependence statements express reliance on some person or thing (an agency, authority, etc.) external to the membership. Behaviors included in this category are: appeals for support or direction from the leader, looking for leader approval, undue attention to the leader, expressing reliance on outside authorities, expressing reliance on structure, procedure or tradition, expressing group weakness and fear of

---

[4] For a detailed development of this material see: Dorothy Stock and Herbert A. Thelen. *Emotional Dynamics and Group Culture*. Washington, D.C.: National Training Laboratories, 1958.

trying things, has misgivings, expresses doubt in a manner that seeks support from the leader, seeks permission from leader, seeks aid and advice from leader, authority or tradition, etc.

Counter-dependency statements express a concern over threat to personal autonomy. The basic dynamic is that the individual has powerful needs for dependency but he over-denies their existence. Behaviors included in this category are: strong displays of independence, insistence on the rights of individuals, questioning of leader's authority, tradition and authorities, overly self-assertive, dramatizes problems of status and authority, self-exalting, interrupting leaders, ridiculing and undermining leadership, procedures and traditions, etc.

These six emotional states or emotionalities operate at the interpersonal contact level. They are modes by which an individual relates to another individual, subgroup, or the group as a whole. They are the delivery styles an individual may use to communicate his concerns and his knowledge. An inspection of the categories readily reveals the approach-avoidance polarity. There are three modes of approach: fight, pairing and dependency. There are three modes of avoidance: flight, counter-pairing, and counter-dependency.

Again, examples may be employed to illustrate this system of categorizing behaviors.

A student teacher may say to his supervisor in the course of a conference:

1. "Yes, I think you are right, I did move in too quickly." Here is a pairing statement and as far as we are able to categorize from an isolated statement a Level 3 work statement.

2. "I think we should take my lesson plan up first, don't you?" This would appear to be a dependency statement and Level 2 work.

It should be obvious that to isolate an interaction utterance makes the coding of the particular interaction utterance difficult. In most instances coding an utterance depends on the context and previous utterances.

Information Channel

There are coding systems in existence which are designed to categorize interactions which occur in small groups. These existing systems in one way or another do not meet the demands of the proposed interaction model. Some systems are only concerned with certain aspects of the information channel (8: 12). The system developed by Bales (1) and later the work of Borgatta (2) do treat directly the communication flow of small interaction groups. Their systems, however, combine the social-emotional categories within the same system as the work categories. The present proposed interaction model attempts to separate these two dimensions on the basis that the social-emotional and the informational subject matters of an interacting group occur simultaneously. This cannot be tested either in Bales' or Borgatta's system.

There is a serious omission in Bales' coding system which can be noted also in the other interaction coding systems. It is the failure of the system to code the target's reaction to the initiator's act unless it is directly and openly expressed. It is possible to observe readily the target's acceptance of an initiator's act when, for instance, he augments the initiator's contribution. The target may not give any codeable act showing agreement, but it is clearly evident that the agreement is embedded in the target's contribution to the initiator's act.

It should also be pointed out that recognizing the agreement tells us very little. It is when we examine the agreement which occurs on the information channel along with the simultaneous codings on the delivery and motivation channels that we may be able to form a defensible explanation for the particular patterns of behavior. For example, it may be found that agreement between two individuals occurs when the initiator gives pairing behaviors.

It is evident from the agreement that if a coding system is designed to categorize interactions, then it is necessary for such a system to report at some level the interaction nature of the acts. It is not sufficient to report the sequence of acts using categories that treat each act as a completely separate entity. The nature of the entity may be determined from context, as is true in Bales' system, but the coding does not directly report the sequential relation of one act to another. It seems only logical in the study of interaction in small groups that the nature of the sequential relations should be categorized whenever possible.

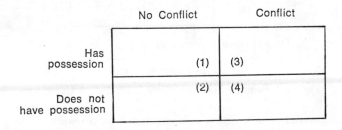

The reception of information has two dimensions. One dimension may be designated as the possession of information dimension. The other may be designated as the conflictual dimension of information. A simple grid diagrams the interrelations of these two dimensions.

A single piece of information may be categorized to one of the four cells. One has or does not have a particular piece of information which is being communicated. The particular piece of information is regarded as not being in conflict with any other piece of information or it is regarded as being in conflict. We act differently according to the cell to which the information has been classified. The types of acts coded to each of the four cells of the matrix may be briefly identified as follows: (a) The information is perceived as Type 1, the target (the individual receiving the information) agrees and/or supports the initiator's contribution. (b) The information is perceived as Type 2, the target may accept the contribution or he may seek more information. His behavior is not rejection or fault finding but a withheld judgment until sufficient additional information is provided. (c) The information is perceived as Type 3, the target will reject the information. (d) The information is perceived as Type 4, the target will question the contribution with the intent of finding some defect in the information.

Only overt responses of the target to an initiator's acts are coded.

There is the cognitive aspect of information. It includes the knowledge of specifics, of ways and means, and of universals.[5] These three aspects which may be employed to categorize information are combined with the reception dimension to form a three dimensional matrix as shown below.

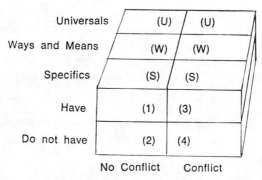

Figure 4. Schema Showing Basic Information Categories

[5] The material in this section is largely based on the work of the committee that produced the volume: Benjamin S. Bloom and D. R. Krathwohl. *Taxonomy of Educational Objectives. Cognitive Domain.* New York: David McKay Co., Inc., 1956.

There is yet one further type of information which is communicated. This type can collectively be referred to as the evaluative aspect. A comment may be specifically a statement of fact without any perceivable evaluative connotations. It is equally possible to transmit an evaluative comment in the form of a statement of fact. The context of a situation and the inflections of voice and mannerism communicate the former message while the flat words communicate the second message. This realization modifies the matrix by building into it the evaluative domain. This is achieved by placing it as a core within the matrix as shown in Figure 5.

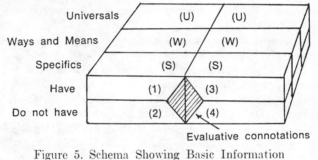

Figure 5. Schema Showing Basic Information
Categories and Evaluative Connotations

The shaded area represents the evaluative domain. It runs through all cells. Thus, it is possible to classify a statement as IUE (have, not in conflict, universal evaluative).

Statements which do not pertain to the subject matter content of the group's agenda are coded as irrelevant.

In summary, I have covered a great deal of material in my paper. Many issues and points of clarification have been unavoidably, hastily glossed over. This was necessary in order that the model in its entirety could be presented.

I am actively testing the model in two projects now under way. One study is investigating the decision-making processes of teaching teams. The other is examining the interpersonal dynamics of leaderless groups in adult education. Hopefully, data from these studies will either support the interaction model presented here, or suggest ways in which it should be modified.

References

1. Robert F. Bales. *Interaction Process Analysis*. Cambridge: Addison-Wesley Press, Inc., 1951.

2. Edgar F. Borgatta. "A Systematic Study of Interaction Process Scores, Peer and Self-Assessments, Personality and Other Variables." *Group Psychology Monograph* 65: 219-91; May 1962.

3. Robert D. Boyd. "Basic Motivation of Adults in Non-Credit Programs." *Journal of Adult Education* 11: 92-98; 1961.

4. Robert D. Boyd. "Ego-Stage Development of School-Age Children." *Journal of Experimental Education* 39 (3): 249-58; Spring 1964.

5. Erik H. Erikson. *Childhood and Society*. New York: W. W. Norton and Co., Inc., 1950.

6. Erik H. Erikson. "Identity and the Life Cycle." Monograph, *Psychological Issues,* Volume 1, Number 1. New York: International University Press, 1959.

7. Otto Fenichel. *The Psycholoanalytical Theory of Neurosis*. New York: W. W. Norton and Co., Inc., 1945.

8. Ned A. Flanders. *Interaction Analysis in the Classroom*. (Revised.) Ann Arbor: University of Michigan, 1964.

9. Robert J. Havighurst. *Human Development and Education*. New York: Longmans, Green and Company, 1953.

10. Dorothy Stock and Herbert A. Thelen. *Emotional Dynamics and Group Culture*. Washington, D.C.: National Training Laboratories, 1958.

11. Herbert A. Thelen and Associates. *Methods for Studying Work and Emotionality in Group Operation*. Chicago: University of Chicago Press, 1954. (Mimeographed.)

12. John Withall. "An Objective Measurement of a Teacher's Classroom Interaction." *Journal of Educational Psychology* 47 (4): 203-12; April 1956.

Effects of Supervisor's Knowledge of Student Teacher Personality Evaluations[1]

Thomas A. Ringness

THE problem we shall be concerned with in this paper is simply this: "If a supervisor of student teachers knows at the beginning of the semester something of the personality characteristics of his charges, is he therefore more able to help them than if he did not have this information?"

This is essentially a question as to whether the supervisor is clearer than he otherwise would be concerning the reasons for certain behaviors of his student teachers, and is therefore clearer as to how to reinforce their desirable acts or to change their behaviors which he feels should be changed. But there are a number of other questions which enter into this deceptively simple postulation.

For example, there is always the problem of whether "personality information" relayed to the supervisor is accurate, germane and comprehensive. That is, is the supervisor told useful things about his student teachers? A second question is whether "personality information" is at all predictive of teaching behavior. A third question is whether the supervisor is in a position to change anything about the student teacher. A fourth question is concerned with ways of bringing about desired changes. And fifth and sixth questions are raised concerning the nature of behavior desired by the supervisor, whether it should be required of the student teacher; and seventh, how can one tell what changes have occurred. Questions such as these pose no end of research, as well as practical problems, as we shall see.

This paper will be divided into the areas of the rationale and some

[1] Based in part upon Project S-035, Office of Education, U.S. Department of Health, Education, and Welfare.

theoretical considerations behind our study; we will present some data and some examples; and then will discuss the problems of working in this area and a few implications for future procedures. I shall primarily refer to a study done by Eleanore A. Larson, now at the University of Rochester, and myself, with senior students and supervisors of an elementary teacher training program at the University of Wisconsin during the academic year 1964-65.

Rationale

My position, in regard to personality theory, is much like that of Gordon Allport, in that I can see advantages in many points of view. I suppose I lean most closely to what some have called a *transactional approach* between the individual and his environment. Let us see how this works out:

It is self-evident that one's personality enters into the development of behavior patterns in a number of ways. This is another way of saying that, unlike the reflexes and instincts of lower animals, human behavior is not a simple connection between stimulus and response, but that mediational processes are important. Among those processes are factors in perception, motivation, attitudes toward self and others, emotional adjustment, prior learning, state of health, intellectual aptitude, and so on. Thus what one attends to in the environment, how he interprets what he senses, his choices of behavioral response, his goals, and even what he perceives as positive or negative reinforcements for his behavior are directly related to various personality characteristics.

Yet these very factors which I have mentioned are, for the most part, learned, and learned over a period of time, the most important part of which may be the early developmental years. At least in the beginning, one's behaviors come about because they are environmentally reinforced or not; later, reinforcement may be internal, in terms of one's goals, value systems, and expectations of self.

I trust this has not seemed peripheral to the reader. This point of view is central to our study, because it suggests that personality characteristics, although highly stable, can be changed; further, they can be changed by others. This is the only justification for making a study in which we are concerned with whether various people know the personality characteristics of others.

Now, the literature supplies a large bibliography of research studies concerning personality characteristics of teachers. Many studies have been devoted to trying to predict good teachers on the basis of their possession of certain personality attributes. Others have been concerned with comparing personality traits of teachers with those of other selected groups, presumably to see whether teachers are "a race apart." If you are familiar with Gage, *Handbook of Research on Teaching*,[2] you may sometime wish to refer to Getzels and Jackson's chapter for a fine résumé of much of this literature. Almost all existing clinical tests and instruments have been employed with teachers, to the point where the authors suggest that it almost seems that when a new test comes along, somebody automatically says, "Let's try it on teachers."

Unfortunately, despite a great amount of research effort, little fruit has been borne. Getzels and Jackson tell us that:

. . . many of the studies so far have not produced significant results. Many others have produced only pedestrian findings. For example, it is said after the usual inventory tabulation that good teachers are friendly, cheerful, sympathetic, and morally virtuous rather than cruel, depressed, unsympathetic, and morally depraved. But when this has been said, not very much that is especially useful has been revealed.[3]

Then they comment extensively upon problems of doing research relating teacher personality to effective teaching behavior, and conclude that too many studies have simply been a relatively blind hunt for characteristics that differentiate good from poor teachers. What is needed, they feel, is *theory* of *how* personality characteristics may be related to teaching success. Thus, when studies are based upon the postulation of relationships between characteristics and effectiveness, it may be possible to get some useful answers. Empiricism, *per se*, has not been very helpful.

Before we look at the design of our study, I would like to mention briefly the problem of criterion variables, since this has been a rock upon which many research ships have foundered. Those readers who are faced with the daily problem of evaluating teachers know only too well that it is difficult to describe the excellent teacher (although almost any child or parent is adept at describing the poorer ones). But any criterion of teaching success is based upon value judgments.

Teaching

It would be possible at this point to get into an involved discussion. I shall bypass the literature (the reader can find it in Barr, Ryans, Gage,

---

[2] N. L. Gage, editor. *Handbook of Research on Teaching*. Chicago: Rand McNally & Company, 1963.

[3] J. W. Getzels and P. W. Jackson. "The Teacher's Personality and Characteristics." *Handbook of Research on Teaching*. N. L. Gage, editor. Chicago: Rand McNally & Company, 1963. p. 574.

and other sources) by simply taking the position that we have taken. We were primarily interested in the nature of teacher-pupil interaction. To attempt to assess this view, we employed the instrument developed by Flanders and Amidon.

We started with the premise that effective modern teaching goes far beyond helping the pupil attain subject matter skills and content. There must also be significant changes in pupils, in motives, attitudes, social perceptions and skills, and in orientations toward themselves and others. Excellent teachers seek to help pupils to gain independence, acceptance of responsibility, and to encourage self-actualization. They try to encourage divergent as well as convergent thinking, and hope that children will learn to solve personal and social, as well as academic problems. They also hope children will learn to be creative, evaluative, critical in thinking, and selective.

We felt that too much teaching may be oriented toward supplying information to pupils, and too little to helping children learn to formulate problems, pick and choose from information, and find ways to apply it. We felt that too frequently children are encouraged to be quite blindly conforming, and to follow teacher directions too assiduously, hence to become too dependent upon the teacher. I can document that this does take place at the junior high school level, since two recently completed studies showed that bright boys feel that the characterization of the model pupil favored by most teachers is one of docility and conformity, rather than of intellectual liveliness, stimulation, questioning, and independent thinking. The boys tended to feel that the teachers resented the pupil who dared to question, disagree, or "think differently." (These studies, by the way, also suggest that many pupils resist this norm, and that this is one reason for disciplinary problems, underachievement, and school dropouts.)

To teach in ways that favor pupil's self-development would seem to require teachers who are pupil-oriented. Frequently this may mean indirect control, in Amidon's terminology. (This does not invariably follow, of course, for the kind of control demanded must depend upon the purposes of the lesson and the nature of the classroom situation. However, the pupil-oriented teacher must provide ways for pupils to think and act independently, to be divergent as well as convergent, and to be creative.) The attitude and subsequent teacher behaviors, we felt, should be those of helping pupils foster their own problem solving and other skills. The activities should be largely those of the pupil, rather than the teacher. In a word, teachers may not only be too dominating in the classroom, and too directive, but they may do too much of the work and accept too much of the responsibility for what the pupil learns.

The aim in helping student teachers was therefore that of helping them become as pupil-oriented as consonant with teacher responsibilities. We hoped they would accept this as their goal, and that supervisors would also feel this way.

Personality Attributes

Let us look at the teachers' characteristics. What motives, needs, personality traits, or other qualities must the teacher have, if he is to be truly pupil-oriented? How will these underlying qualities be manifest in teaching behavior?

Wallen and Travers, in Gage's *Handbook of Research on Teaching*, looked at patterns of teaching generated by the teacher's own needs or motives. They noted, for example, that the lecture method of teaching holds sway in many classrooms, not because it is based on scientific knowledge of learning principles, but perhaps because some teachers have a "need to talk" in the classroom, hence rationalize their use of lecturing. Although this is probably an oversimplification, they suggest that some teachers talk because it is a way of controlling pupils, or because it is a means of achieving recognition, or perhaps because some teachers are compulsive about imparting information.

Similarly, we might feel that authoritarian teachers may have a need and a tendency to dominate others. They may need to demonstrate authority because of basic insecurity. Teachers with exhibitionistic tendencies might demonstrate this in the classroom by flamboyant behavior, attempting to entertain pupils by putting on a show. Teachers with strong unmet affectional needs might lean on pupils for such affection, having pets, being permissive, expressing undue interest in pupils' private lives, or keeping them too close to the teacher.

If we accept that underlying needs or motives do govern behavior, it would seem to be important to have some idea of the nature of such needs or motives in order that supervisors can interpret the teaching behavior they observe. It is well known, of course, that a given overt behavior can signify different things depending upon motives; equally, a given motive can result in different kinds of behavior. I suppose I am really referring to the need for a supervisor to employ Ojemann's "causal approach" in supervision, just as he asks the teacher to employ it in regard to children.

I must introduce one other point; then we will move to a briefing on the design of our study. Rogers has remarked that teachers and therapists are alike in that both must be congruent, accepting, and interested in knowing as much as possible about client or pupil. The concept of congruence means that the teacher must be himself: he must reflect his true feelings and attitudes in the classroom. He must be aware of and able to accept his feelings and emotions. The teacher therefore cannot play a role. This would be sensed by pupils, and a falseness and distrust in teacher-pupil relations would result.

We can now see a rationale for attempting to deal with personality attributes of the student teacher. Not only will the supervisor be presumably more able to govern behavior desirably, since he is dealing not with specifics but with underlying causal generalities, but he must find ways to help the student teacher be aware of his own characteristics. The student must become aware of his own shortcomings; being aware, he can find ways to overcome them. Equally, a teacher should be aware of his desirable characteristics; in this event, he may capitalize upon them. Thus the insecure teacher can be helped to find ways to become secure. The dominant teacher can be helped to see the dangers of overdominance of pupils, and be on guard against this tendency.

My experience with supervisors leads me to believe that many of them do not deal with, or even have much understanding of, the personalities of student teachers. Their time is too frequently spent in making suggestions about specific teacher behaviors, subject content, or teaching methodology.

Design of the Study

The study conducted by Dr. Larson and myself took place at the University of Wisconsin, covering both semesters of the academic year 1964-65. During the first semester, 32 elementary education student teachers and four supervisors were studied; during the second semester there were 46 student teachers and four supervisors (of which there were three repeating and one new supervisor).

Finding almost no controlled experiments in the literature dealing with student teachers and supervision, we decided to attempt such a study. Needless to say, full control in the laboratory sense is almost impossible in the field situation. Accordingly we employed randomization of subjects in an attempt to minimize the effects of uncontrollable factors.

Student teachers were randomly assigned in equal numbers to each supervisor. They were then also assigned randomly into one of three treatment conditions, as we shall see.

All students were given the same initial treatment. They were asked to respond to the Edwards Personal Preference Schedule (EPPS), the

California Psychological Inventory (CPI), ten Thematic Apperception Test (TAT) cards, and were interviewed by a psychologist. Basing his impressions upon these data, the psychologist then prepared thumbnail sketches of the student teachers, in which their salient characteristics were mentioned. An attempt was made to predict areas of the teaching process in which they might have success or which might pose problems. Suggestions as to how treatment might be instituted were also provided.

The control group received no feedback concerning their thumbnail sketches until the end of the semester, after student teaching had been completed. Since they repeatedly heard experimental groups discuss their experiences, one can imagine that they awaited their own interpretations with considerable anticipation. Because these girls were essentially high calibre persons, interpretations tended to be somewhat flattering and the interpretation session received by the experimental groups got to be known as a "fun session." I guess there was also considerable speculation, and even a little betting concerning what would be told to them later.

Experimental Group One (E-1) consisted of student teachers who received immediate feedback and counseling concerning findings, and whose University supervisors (with student permission) also received this same information.

Experimental Group Two (E-2) consisted of student teachers who received immediate feedback, but whose supervisors were *not* given information.

The thought was that supervisors would work in a different way with students about whom they had information. It was also the notion that students who had information but whose supervisors had not, would be more able to help themselves than the control group, always assuming that they accepted the sketches as being accurate and realistic.

Before discussing other procedures, I will introduce three thumbnail sketches that were developed, to show the reader something of the information we provided:

Nancy

Nancy was seen as secure, well-integrated, a leader or good follower type. She is sociable and has a good feeling for and understanding of people. She is flexible, probably very creative, stimulating, and spontaneous. She is quite independent, and may not always conform. Nancy is academically competitive, enthused, and forceful. We might describe her as self-actualizing. Nancy mentions a possible M.S. in Guidance or School Psychology. She would be excellent, since she can relate well to children and others, and is accepting, intuitive and understanding. She will make an excellent, creative teacher, and will probably be pupil-centered.

Yet she will maintain control and efficient direction of the classroom activities. She is strong enough to prevent discipline problems, but will be free and flexible. She needs only to be challenged and given opportunity to act "on her own." Nancy should be one of our best student-teachers.

To indicate whether we were accurate in making this appraisal, I offer these subsequent comments by her supervisor:

Nancy is one of my three top students. I thought this before, and I still do. She's exciting to see. The way she can implement the ideas of the kids right on the spot in a part of the lesson without losing the direction of the lesson at all is amazing. She wraps it all up, uses it, and capitalizes upon what they come up with in ways I haven't seen people with lots of experience do. The kids are free to challenge her, but there is respect, order and control. They are taking lots of responsibility for what goes on; they do a lot of the planning; there is much interaction among the pupils, using one another's ideas, using teacher ideas, and so on. There's a lot of this intercommunication—it's outstanding. And she knows the children. She showed me a picture of the class and went right down the line telling me, "We have this kind of situation in the home, this child we have tried to treat in this way, but this kid, it doesn't work so well with him so we do that instead," and so on. She knows these children well, and can use her knowledge right on the spot. It's unusual for a student-teacher.

But that was a "top" girl. Maybe we did not do as well with some of the others. For example, let us look at Sharon:

Sharon

Sharon has high needs for achievement, order and succorance. She likes the support of others, and seems a bit insecure. She has a high need to achieve, but is a bit wary, defensive, and may not have close relationships with others. She is low in acceptance of responsibility, in dominance, affiliation and nurturance. She may be a reasonably "standard" teacher, but she may not pay sufficient attention to pupil needs and may find it hard to form good relationships with them. She will probably be somewhat overstructured, a bit rigid, too closely planned. We need to help her pay more attention to the pupils, and less to herself. Can we help her loosen up?

Sharon's supervisor remarked:

I saw Sharon's arithmetic class. The whole class got a bad grade and she blamed the whole class for it. She said the whole class failed and, "Well, this was all fourth grade arithmetic and it's all their fault," and so on. Well, it *was* review. Perhaps it might be a good idea to ask them what they had wrong and put it on the board and discuss it? She thought perhaps it might be right. I have discussed with her since I first came out such things as the idea that you do not give kids isolated vocabulary words for reading and just put them on the board. But every time I'm out there, they're still on the board—isolated—and I've given up on that.

I once said to Sharon, "I feel you are somewhat rigid with these children. Why?" She smiled and said, "That's a hard one to answer. I suppose this is the way it's set up, maybe; this is the school atmosphere, and this is why." I said "Do you think your own classroom will be different?" She thought it would be. I don't look for any change, but at least she does recognize that I feel she is rigid in her teaching.

And one more, Judy:

Judy

Judy was seen as restless, frustrated, and unable to control aggressive feelings. She does not relate well to others, and shows negative feeling tone. She resents pressure to conform, and has some unusual interests and ideas. She would like to be praised, but is essentially passive, retiring, inhibited, and lacking in confidence. Judy is very self-centered, defensive, resentful, and rebellious. She is moody, impatient, and manipulative. We suggested that she request student counseling, but she would not accept this suggestion, denying any validity in test and interview results.

She was expected to have difficulties relating to children and others; she is not highly motivated to teach, and does not appreciate the feelings and needs of others. She was expected to have a poor reaction to any pressures put upon her. She needs encouragement, and we need to get her to pay more attention to children. She needs careful watching.

Her supervisor remarked:

I've tried everything with Judy, but things have blown up again. I went on another trip to see her and talked with her and tried to find what was the matter; I felt she was so down in the dumps I took her out for lunch. I think if you say "Judy, this is not good" you get nowhere with her. Her cooperating teacher had been taking some of the work away from her, because she wasn't doing anything. Her trouble comes partly from last year. They tried to steer her out of teaching. And now she doesn't know whether she *can* teach. She doesn't have rapport with the children, or with the other teachers. She's very aloof. She doesn't want to face up to herself.

Now, having provided feedback—or not—we proceeded to collect other data. For example, we collected self and ideal-self card sorts from the students at the beginning and end of the semester. These were based on EPPS and CPI variables. In addition, the supervisors and the psychologist made card sorts for each student in regard to self and ideal-self.

We also had weekly anecdotes from the students about their work and how things were going, and we had the supervisors in to discuss the students after each visit. For those about whom the supervisors had information, we discussed how their problems might be tackled.

Because we had argued that experimental treatment should show up in supervisors' abilities to help students become more pupil-oriented, we used Flanders' technique to see how they interacted in their classrooms, and how they changed during student teaching. We made four observations on selected classroom discussion situations, for each student teacher. It was hoped that we would find movement from direct to indirect control of pupils in classroom discussion most apparent in E-1, with feedback to both student and supervisor, next most apparent in E-2, with feedback to student only, and less in the control group.

Differences in Supervisory Tactics

It is at this point that the application of social learning theory principles becomes important. The work of Dollard and Miller, Bandura and Walters, and others has shown the usefulness of this theory in changing behavior of all kinds, including emotional behavior, and motivational factors. Social learning theory does not assume that there are no mediating variables between stimulus and response; but it does emphasize the importance of reinforcement in governing behavior. Further, Bandura and Walters emphasize the importance of modeling and imitation. A supervisor who employed social learning theory principles would therefore try to provide the student teacher with an effective model, and to reinforce appropriate student behaviors. On the other hand, inappropriate behaviors would be subjected to negative reinforcement, or if possible, allowed to extinguish through non-reinforcement or be superseded by alternative, more appropriate behavior.

Let us consider one of the EPPS variables as an example of this approach, as compared to a perhaps more traditional approach. We might take the variable termed *aggression* for our example. After all, teachers are not supposed to be aggressive—at least not toward pupils, or for that matter toward parents, principals and superintendents.

Now, according to Edwards, high score on any variable indicates a high need, but it does not say whether that person exhibits that need in a particular way. So a student teacher high in aggression might simply *wish* to be more aggressive, or might actually *be* more aggressive. Further, if aggressive, it is possible that he is aggressive in a "nice way," e.g., competitive, or fighting social evils. Or he may sublimate, try to repress aggressive tendencies, or turn aggressive tendencies against himself, that is, be punitive toward self. The reason for the interview with the student at the beginning of the semester is partly to get a better idea of whether the student *is* or *would like to be* aggressive.

But let us assume that the student teacher really is aggressive. He is punitive, hostile, sarcastic, blaming, and frequently openly angry. He may, like a teacher I remember from high school, even throw things such as chalk or erasers at pupils who did not please him.

Now, some might suggest that we allow this aggressive person to get rid of the need by gratifying it. That is, we would help the student release hostile feelings in legitimate, socially acceptable ways—perhaps by hammering the piano, in athletics, by writing letters to the editor, or in other ways.

However, Bandura and Walters would think that aggressive behavior is modeled; it is learned, probably by a combination of imitation and reinforcement. Thus they would prefer to have all aggressive acts either not reinforced, or negatively reinforced. The supervisor, finding an aggressive student, might punish the aggressive behavior, or he might try to reduce the aggression-producing stimuli in the student's environment, or he might try to teach the aggressor to relax. Nonaggressive models might help, so that such a student teacher might be placed with a patient, understanding, nonaggressive cooperating teacher. Further, the student's nonaggressive acts could be positively reinforced.

Or, take the need for succorance. Essentially this is a form of dependency. Edwards describes it as a need to have others provide help when in trouble, to seek encouragement from others, to have others be kindly, to have others be sorry for one, and the like. In a word, the need to be "babied." This seems to reflect a basic insecurity.

Now, we all like to have others succor us, especially if we are feeling low. But one of our girls told the supervisor that "supervisors are supposed to be supportive, especially of her, since she had an inferiority complex." A social learning theorist would argue that if one were supportive of such a person, he might be reinforcing the need and related dependent behavior. In a word, you do not make a person more self sufficient by constantly providing more support. You try, instead, gradually to wean him by withdrawing support and making him stand on his own two feet. Of course, you are careful not to try to make him over all at once—you move somewhat gradually. You also try to reinforce any strong, mature, independent behavior, and withhold unnecessary aid and sympathy.

This approach was used in advising supervisors about working with their student teachers.

It is possible, of course, for supervisors to gain considerable knowledge of their student teachers without having psychological test data and interpretations provided them. Indeed, one of the interesting outcomes of this study was the appearance of a sort of "new look" in supervision, in which the supervisors' topics for discussion with the psychologist, and even their choice of vocabulary, began to evolve about personality characteristics of the students. Interest in personality dimensions fostered concerning group E-1 seemed to spill over to the ways supervisors looked at all students. However, it is true that they were somewhat clearer about characteristics of students about whom they had feedback.

Advance personality information should help in two ways—it should allow a head start with the student teacher, and it should provide for less speculation and fumbling in trying to decide what a given behavior stems from. Assuming such information is helpful to supervisors, would it be helpful to students?

It should be noted that in feedback interviews students were not simply told "you are so-and-so and thus-and-such." Rather, they learned that their test scores might be high on certain dimensions and that we were interested in exploring with them what this might mean; in this way both student and psychologist might gain a better idea of the real nature of the student. For example, a student with high exhibition needs would be probed to see whether he actually tried to take the center of the stage, say at a party, or as cheerleader, performing in public, and so on. Or did he act this way only in intimate groups? Or was this only a desire on his part? This was particularly true in regard to the EPPS; the CPI simply discusses one's behavior, so in regard to its findings, we simply asked students to react to them.

If the student did, indeed, have exhibitionistic tendencies, it was suggested that this could be utilized for good. He could be a highly stimulating teacher. But on the other hand, he might need to guard against monopolizing the center of the classroom stage, thus really performing for the pupils and not permitting them opportunity to express ideas of their own. Such ideas were explored with the E-1 and E-2 groups.

The following student-teacher comments, obtained from written reactions during the semester, indicate that it worked for some of them, at least—or so they said:

I've been aware that I was too anxious to do all the talking in the classroom, and that this probably reflected a need to structure everything so it would go well. I'm working on this, trying to let the children come through more, with their own ideas.

You told me I probably liked to be the center of attention. How true. But I know this isn't good, so I'm making sure to call on the kids; especially those who are too shy to raise their hands.

Yes, my so-called dominance is really a cover-up. But I've learned not to be afraid of the children—they need you so much, at this age, and are really no threat. So I'm gaining confidence in myself, and I can be more like I really am.

So it can be done. Unfortunately our data does not give us enough clues as to how often students made use of our comments. We saw them change, in many ways, but whether it was the study, the supervisors, the cooperating teachers, just plain experience, or what, was very hard to figure out.

Findings of the Study

First, we intercorrelated the various card-sorts—the self and ideal-self sorts made at the beginning and end of the semester by the students, and those by the supervisor and psychologist. Considering the small sample size we worked with, it was surprising how well the card sorts correlated. On certain sorts, such as the EPPS variable called *order*, we found 28 out of 45 correlations significant at the 5 percent level, and for *autonomy*, 37 out of 45 significant r's. Poorest intercorrelations were with some CPI variables, which we attributed to the comparative difficulty of writing good card sort items from CPI descriptions of variables; for the EPPS, we could take items almost directly from the descriptive part of the manual.

One might wonder whether there were more significant intercorrelations with E-1 or E-2 groups as compared with the control group. For what it is worth, the answer is "no." Thus we cannot say that providing information to supervisors about certain students helped them to describe the students more as the students saw themselves, or that information provided the students enabled them to see themselves more as others saw them. That is, we would have expected the final card-sorts of students to look more like those of supervisors and psychologists for the E-1 and E-2 groups than for the controls, but this did not occur. We think there are a number of reasons for this: for example, I have already stated that the study seemed to orient supervisors to looking at personality traits for all groups, rather than just those of the E-1 group. This spill-over seems to have sharpened perceptions and focused observations which contributed equally to all groups.

We found student teachers to be quite consistent within themselves. Thus self and ideal-self correlated highly; initial and final sorts correlated highly. We can draw two tentative conclusions from this. First, that most student teachers have stabilized notions about themselves and that these do not particularly change under conditions of treatment which we prescribed. And, second, most student teachers accept themselves, in that self and ideal-self sorts are highly correlated. A peripheral finding was that Edwards seemed to be absolutely correct when he stated that the EPPS had pretty well overcome the factor of social

desirability in responses to his instrument. The self and ideal-self correlations were high, but the EPPS correlated higher with the self than
with the ideal-self sorts.

The psychologist made two card-sorts concerning each student
teacher. The first was based on test and interview data only. The second
was based on anecdotal information supplied during the semester by
the students and supervisors. The first sort corresponded well with the
test results and card-sorts of the student teachers. The sort based on
anecdotes corresponded well with supervisors' sorts. But, sad to say,
the supervisor (and psychologist) sorts corresponded much less well
with student sorts.

This may be interpreted in several ways. We can argue quite safely
that motives or traits do not necessarily translate directly into observable
behavior. We can call attention to the relatively limited opportunities
for supervisors to observe students, and also to the relatively structured
situations in which the observations occurred. Yet perhaps even more
important was the ability (or lack of ability) of the supervisor to
assess the student—the supervisors were highly variable in this regard.
One supervisor was found to be completely content- and method-oriented.
Her reliability ratings in the use of the Flanders technique were low
at the start and got poorer with time. Other signs, e.g., discussion with
the psychologist, suggested that she was completely unable to empathize
with and understand students' behavior. Another supervisor, trained in
guidance and counseling, was highly empathetic. The others were some-
where in between. On the whole, we were pleased, considering the size
of the sample and nature of the data, to do as well as we did—the significant correlations were far better than chance would have anticipated.

Highest intercorrelations among all sorts included the EPPS variables
of deference, order, autonomy, intraception, succorance, dominance,
abasement, endurance, and change. Those least correlated included
achievement, exhibition, affiliation, nurturance, heterosexuality, and aggression. It seems likely that, for the most part, the former variables
would be more observable in the classroom and informal contact of
supervisor and student.

CPI variables most intercorrelated included sociability, social presence, responsibility, communality, flexibility, and femininity. These, too,
are quite observable in the classroom and informal contact.

In looking at CPI and EPPS data, we performed analyses of vari-
ance between the groups, by test, for each variable. There were no
statistically significant results—within-group variability was such that
it overshadowed between-group or between-test variability. However,

this does not surprise us much. This is one of the problems with using group data in comparison with analyzing individual cases. Thus, one girl might be high in dominance and lower at the end of the semester, but in the same group a girl who was originally low in dominance but gained at the end of the semester might be present—in a sense, these two would cancel each other out.

We did find nonsignificant but interesting results for the groups as a whole. The girls, over the semester, seemed to turn out somewhat lower in nurturance, and somewhat higher in dominance. They also turned out a little lower in femininity. Apparently student teachers become more "hard-boiled" as a result of their experiences. The sweet, idealistic girls with whom we started have found that they must become more controlling than they had originally been, and that they must recognize that not all children are always "nice," or "cute," and sometimes discipline must be enforced in not so lady-like ways.

Turning to the Flanders scale, we had given our supervisors extensive training and had achieved some good reliabilities, both between and within raters. We asked student teachers to set up discussions, 20 minutes long, based on social studies. Because the girls were spread from first to sixth grades, we could not achieve comparable content and level. Amidon, I believe, considers this essential if real comparison were to be drawn between groups. However, we did feel that randomization of students might be helpful to some extent in overcoming this problem.

Nevertheless, it will not surprise the reader to learn that once again, within-group variability, and variability from observation to observation among students overshadowed between-group differences. In fact, one thing that amazed us was how differently the same student teacher behaved from the first to the fourth observation. There was frankly no consistency. These students, at least, had not formed typical patterns of classroom interaction. Further, they did not get more pupil-oriented with time. The same inconsistency held. When queried about this, their usual answer was that the particular classroom situation was at fault— children restless, or visitor upset the routine, or content really not suitable for discussion, etc.

We found one other problem—that is, that we could quite well assess (we thought) the nature of teacher-pupil interaction, but that many apparently "good" interactions were not germane or else frequently left the track. This is the old problem of having a good discussion bearing little fruit in learning as compared with a poor discussion but which might have some significant outcomes.

One other kind of data should be noted at this point. You might ask, "If the psychologist suggested a given girl to be dominant and that she should try to tone this down, how did she change? Or, if a girl was seen as insecure, was she helped?"

This sort of information comes from individual analyses of students' folders. I shall offer a sample or two, only:

SHARON: Seen as low in responsibility and low in dominance. Picked up an average of 17 T-score points from 1st to 2nd administration.

JUDY: Seen as high in aggression, low in endurance, high in succorance, improved an average of 10 T-score points. She also became slightly less aggressive (resentful) but 11 points higher in deference.

NANCY: A little more autonomous, a little less abasing, and a little more aggressive. She was the girl whom we saw as a top student, so we had recommended only that she be allowed to try things out for herself. She also became somewhat more interested in heterosexual activities—but no surprise—she married in June!

Problems, Conclusions, Recommendations

I shall first suggest that this study was a highly enjoyable one, not only to the researchers, but to the student teachers and supervisors. When we began, there was some feeling of threat, which quickly appeared to evaporate. We also enjoyed excellent cooperation from all concerned.

I think a main finding was that the students and supervisors became much more sensitive than before to personality characteristics, not only of themselves, but of their pupils—and how these characteristics might be reflected in the classroom. For my part, when I discuss the concept of the "causal approach," the study of the pupils, and the like with my educational psychology and mental health students, I shall be very tempted to employ tests such as these, with interpretations, to sensitize my students in this way. We found supervisors talking about rigidity, endurance, passiveness, and similar terms, not only with the psychologist, but with the girls.

I was amazed at the intra-group variability on almost all dimensions. Although these were quite a homogeneous group of girls, compared with a random population their age, the variability on all instruments was surprising. This, plus variability of supervisors, placements, and cooperating teachers, I am sure, accounted largely for the lack of significant between-group findings.

We were much surprised to see how well the EPPS, self, and ideal-self card sorts agreed with each other, and the corresponding CPI variables as well. Apparently student teachers accept themselves quite well, and their opinions of themselves tend to be quite stable. It is interesting to note that in the feedback interview, most girls felt that we had basically said accurate things about them. The errors were more likely to be of omission, rather than of commission.

It was clear that individual students and supervisors working with student teachers were making use of the data. Although results were not always statistically significant, changes in EPPS and CPI from pre- to post-student teaching generally reflected feedback interview data and suggestions, and were in the "right" direction.

We also discovered that Flanders and Amidon are correct in their insistence that comparisons of interaction can only be useful, *other than for teaching purposes,* when situations are carefully controlled. The girls profited from discussion of their scores on the various observations, but we found the data useful only in that way and not for discriminating between groups as a criterion measure.

Some peripheral findings I have not mentioned must include the fact that one girl broke down emotionally at the feedback interview—this was not surprising—her test results showed her to be hanging on the ragged edge. She sought counseling and was referred to the Student Counseling Center, and subsequently was greatly improved and certified for teaching. I am not suggesting that this study or others be made in order to screen students—I think this unethical unless this is frankly made part of policy and is explained to students. I am saying that this was in this instance an added benefit.

On the other hand, one girl, already mentioned, absolutely refused to discuss the test findings, which were also discouraging. She, sadly, nearly failed in her student teaching, but a great many extra hours put in by the supervisor finally bore enough fruit so that she could be safely certified. Two other girls were found to already be in counseling, and were more than happy to discuss their problems with us. The most interesting girl was one whom the psychologist characterized as rather impulsive, deferent, and dependent. He remarked that he thought she should watch that she did not get talked into doing things without too much thought. Her retort was, "Yes, and that includes marriage."

Now, in case any of our readers might be tempted to try something of this sort, let me face them with some problems. I have already mentioned some of these, of course. Here I shall add others.

As to instruments, the EPPS and CPI are objective, and lend themselves to statistical comparisons, and to use with related card-sorts. They have the disadvantage common to all self-report instruments—they can be "cooked" either to show a "good profile" or a "bad profile." We believe we had excellent rapport, and were not amazed at any profile, but the danger does exist. Further, they are limited in both the scales provided, and the interpretation the testee makes from the items. On the other hand, the TAT provides a great deal of useful information, and is sort of free-wheeling, but it is not objective.

I would suggest that, for the trained clinical psychologist, probably the TAT, combined with the interview, provided the best overall pictures of the girls. Furthermore, they enjoyed these more than the paper-and-pencil tests. It is probable, however, that if I were to repeat this as a "for real" study, rather than a pilot study, I would want a lot more background data on the girls. We would need to know some factors that we later accidentally discovered—for example, several of our "insecure" girls were found to be that way because of experiences they had undergone in pre-student teaching laboratory experiences. I would want to know much more than we did know about how they saw themselves. But even more important, perhaps, would be some sort of sociometric measure—to get a better picture of the ways the girls saw each other. We were reasonably accurate in our interpretations, but we could have been better.

Another finding which seems important to me is that I should like much longer time in which to train supervisors, not only in discussing with them how to employ test results, how to work with the girls, and the like, but to gain some common agreement as to objectives of supervision. This is an old bug-bear, I am sure the reader will agree, but it was evident that the supervisors varied greatly in their viewpoints about classroom teaching as well as in ability to empathize and work with the student teachers.

We probably would do better, as I understand is the case in San Francisco State College and at Bank Street College, to make this sort of study much earlier in the girls' careers and to work with them over a longer period. This cannot be done at Wisconsin, however, for in most cases we do not have them until the junior year. I understand further that the trend is now to the senior year or graduate year intern program, meaning that we will see even less of them before their student teaching, hence have less time with which to work with them on these so-called fundamental problems.

We need to give consideration to placing students with cooperating teachers more successfully. One student teacher got severely criticized by her cooperating teacher for certain practices; yet the supervisor commented that the real problem was that "Mrs. X didn't like to see herself up there in front of herself, teaching." Which means that the girl had carbon-copied Mrs. X, who did not recognize this, and criticized the girl for doing what she, herself, set as an example. Since modeling is an important concept in social learning theory, I believe that I would tend to place students with cooperating teachers who had complementary characteristics in most instances. Thus, the passive student might learn from a more outgoing cooperating teacher, the insensitive student teacher might learn from a sensitive cooperating teacher, and so on.

I am also concerned that our University supervisors did not have more time in which to work with the girls. On the average they were able to make about five visits during the student-teaching bloc of time, and part of each visit was given to observations with the Flanders scale. Further, I am not always certain that either the cooperating teacher or the supervisor is adequately trained in supervision, let alone the ability to carry this on as part of a graduate student or full-time teaching load.

Interaction Analysis as a Feedback System in Teacher Preparation

Edmund J. Amidon
and Evan Powell

MANY educators and social scientists have pointed out that supervision is primarily a social process which involves interaction between two or more people. The most important elements of the supervisory relationship appear to be concerned with the ability of supervisors to communicate effectively with teachers. Educators have spoken these words for many years and yet little systematic research has been focused on the study of the supervisory process.

Any study of the improvement of teaching through supervision seems to necessitate a focus on three problem areas:

1. The interaction of the teacher and supervisor as they attempt to discuss what the teacher is doing and how he can improve.

2. The description of interaction between teacher and class which serves as the basis of the supervisory conference.

3. The social skills involved in any group situation, whether it is in a conference, a classroom, or a faculty meeting.

Principles

In order to work on all three of these problems simultaneously, several principles have been examined and used as guideposts in the development of the study reported in this paper.

1. The supervisor must be given a *tool* for assessing the effects of his own behavior on the teacher or student teacher.

This tool was provided by training a group of cooperating teachers in the use of Flanders' System of Interaction Analysis. The teachers were asked to think about the way they interacted with their student teacher while they were having a conference following a classroom observation.

The cooperating teachers were also exposed to role playing situations which allowed them to receive feedback about the extent to which they were producing defensiveness in the student teacher. For these purposes, some of the categories proposed by Blumberg were used.

2. The supervisor must have a *tool* available for objectively describing what the teacher or student teacher does in the classroom.

In order to satisfy this need, each cooperating teacher was given about twenty hours of training in the use of Interaction Analysis. The cooperating teachers were asked to have five conferences during the semester with their student teacher. At this time they would present the student teacher with an interaction matrix.

3. Feedback is essential to the improvement of both teaching and supervisory skills.

This principle was made operational through the use of the interaction matrix. This matrix summarized the data collected through the use of the ten-category system of Interaction Analysis. This matrix enables a teacher to determine how much he talks, how he responds to student talk, and what happens after he asks a question. In one sense the matrix helps a teacher to determine whether or not his teaching intentions are met.

4. Both teachers and supervisors must be free to experiment with those skills which they wish to improve.

This can only be done through providing the appropriate environment in the school and classroom. This is the reason for the training of cooperating teachers. Still, structured role playing enables teachers and supervisors to try out those behaviors which seem to be important to the improvement of their teaching and supervisory skills.

5. The direction of improvement must be arrived at by the teacher with the help of his supervisor.

Implementation of procedures in accordance with this principle resulted in a rather structured approach to the supervisory conference. All cooperating teachers were asked to present the interaction matrix to their student teacher and then let the student teacher decide in which ways he would like to change.

Interaction Analysis

Interaction Analysis has been mentioned here several times, yet not everyone is familiar with it. The Flanders System of Interaction Analysis is an observational procedure which can be used to classify the verbal behavior of teachers and pupils. Using this system, verbal behavior in the classroom is classified into ten category designations. There are seven categories for teacher behavior, four of which are classified as indirect influence. They are: (1) accepting pupil feeling, (2) praising or encouraging, (3) accepting pupil ideas, (4) asking questions. There are three categories of direct teacher influence, which are: (5) giving information or opinion, (6) giving directions, and (7) criticizing. Two categories of pupil talk are used in the system: (8) pupil response to the teacher, and (9) pupil initiated talk. Category 10 is used to indicate silence or confusion. These categories are summarized in Figure 1.

A trained observer notes every verbal behavior as it occurs, and if it persists, puts down the same number every three seconds until there is a change. After a lesson has been categorized, the data collected by the observer must be summarized so that it can be interpreted. This is done by entering the category numbers in the form of tallies into a 10-row by 10-column table called a matrix. The completed matrix gives the observer a picture not only of the percentage of interactions falling in each category but also of the general sequence of responses. Although an exact representation of the sequential time element of the entire lesson is not shown, recording the numbers in the matrix in an overlapping fashion preserves the sequential time element of adjacent numbers. Thus, the researcher might note that praise followed student response about 10 percent of the total lesson time and yet be unable to extract from the matrix whether the praise occurred during the first or last fifteen minutes of the particular lesson. For specific information about sequence the observer relies on his raw data which was initially recorded in a column. The following example is offered to help clarify the use of the matrix.

Suppose that after the observer enters the classroom the following sequence of events takes place. The teacher starts by saying, "Boys and girls, sit down in your seats and take out your workbooks" (category 6). Bill, one of the brighter children, responds to this by saying, "But, Mrs. Adams, I thought you said we were going to have a story this morning" (category 9). The teacher then reacts to Bill by saying, "Bill, you know that you were so noisy today that I decided to punish you by

Teacher Talk	Indirect Influence	1.* *Accepts feeling:* accepts and clarifies the feeling tone of the students in a nonthreatening manner. Feelings may be positive or negative. Predicting and recalling feelings are included. 2.* *Praises or encourages:* praises or encourages student action or behavior. Jokes that release tension, not at the expense of another individual, nodding head or saying "uhhuh?" or "go on" are included. 3.* *Accepts or uses ideas of student:* clarifying, building, or developing ideas or suggestions by a student. As teacher brings more of his own ideas into play, shift to category five. 4.* *Asks questions:* asking a question about content or procedure with the intent that a student answer.
	Direct Influence	5.* *Lecturing:* giving facts or opinions about content or procedure; expressing his own idea; asking rhetorical questions. 6.* *Giving directions:* directions, commands, or orders with which a student is expected to comply. 7.* *Criticizing or justifying authority:* statements intended to change student behavior from nonacceptable to acceptable pattern; bawling someone out; stating why the teacher is doing what he is doing; extreme self-reference.
Student Talk		8.* *Student talk-response:* talk by students in response to teacher. Teacher initiates the contact or solicits student statement. 9.* *Student talk-initiation:* talk by students, which they initiate. If "calling on" student is only to indicate who may talk next, observer must decide whether student wanted to talk. If he did, use this category.
		10.* *Silence or confusion:* pauses, short periods of silence, and periods of confusion in which communication cannot be understood by the observer.

Figure 1. Categories for Interaction Analysis [1]
(Minnesota, 1959)

[1] Edmund J. Amidon and Ned A. Flanders. *The Role of the Teacher in the Classroom: A Manual for Understanding and Improving Teachers' Classroom Behavior.* Minneapolis, Minnesota: Paul S. Amidon & Associates, Inc., 1963. p. 12.

* There is *no* scale implied by these numbers. Each number is classificatory; it designates a particular kind of communication event. To write these numbers down during observation is to enumerate, not to judge a position on a scale.

making you work in your workbooks. I don't like it when you forget these things, Bill" (category 7).

(The observer records two 7's in a row because of the length of the statement.) Then the teacher continues, "Now I think we can forget about the story and get to work in the workbooks. If we do a good job then we will have the story tomorrow." (The first part of the teacher's statement is a 6 and the last part, a 5.) The observer has recorded the following column of numbers, pairing them as shown below:

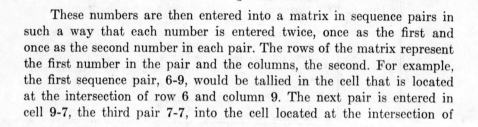

These numbers are then entered into a matrix in sequence pairs in such a way that each number is entered twice, once as the first and once as the second number in each pair. The rows of the matrix represent the first number in the pair and the columns, the second. For example, the first sequence pair, 6-9, would be tallied in the cell that is located at the intersection of row 6 and column 9. The next pair is entered in cell 9-7, the third pair 7-7, into the cell located at the intersection of

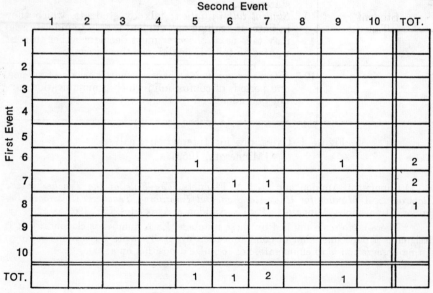

Figure 2. Sample Matrix

row 7 and column 7; etc. Figure 2 shows the actual location of these five tallies in the matrix.

The Study

Objectives

Of course any program, if it is to be replicated, must be part of a research design and have the appropriate controls built into it. The present study is designed as a two-and-a-half year study to test the relationships between the training of cooperating teachers and certain course content, and the behavior and attitudes of student teachers.

The study tests the following hypotheses:

1. Student teachers taught Interaction Analysis are more indirect at the end of their student teaching experience than student teachers not so taught.

2. Student teachers who are taught Interaction Analysis and are supervised by cooperating teachers trained in Interaction Analysis are more indirect at the end of student teaching than student teachers not receiving such training and supervision.

Procedures

General Design. There are two important variables: student teaching course content and the training of the cooperating teacher. The course content for student teachers consists of either traditional learning theory or Interaction Analysis. The cooperating teacher is trained in the use of Interaction Analysis as an observational technique, or receives training in learning theory.

This design makes it possible to treat the influence of two independent variables: the training of cooperating teachers and student teaching course content, upon the dependent variables: ratings of student teachers' teaching effectiveness, attitudes of student teachers, pupil perception of student teacher change, and student teachers' teaching patterns. The four groups are compared with one another to determine whether student teaching course content or the training of the cooperating teacher or a combination of the two has the most significant influence on the dependent variables. The study will be carried on for five successive semesters in order to provide for replication of the experiment.

Group I. Student teachers in this group are taught Interaction Analysis in a two hour a week lecture and a two hour a week laboratory. In addition, they have a two hour a week seminar with their college supervisor in which they can discuss problems they are having in their teaching. The cooperating teacher, using Interaction Analysis, observes the student teacher formally once a week for 30 to 40 minutes, and spends one hour a week discussing the observation with the student.

Cooperating Teacher

		Supervision is done by a cooperating teacher trained in Interaction Analysis	Supervision is done by a cooperating teacher trained in learning theory
Course Content	Interaction Analysis and Seminar	15 Students Group I	15 Students Group II
	Learning Theory and Seminar	15 Students Group III	15 Students Group IV

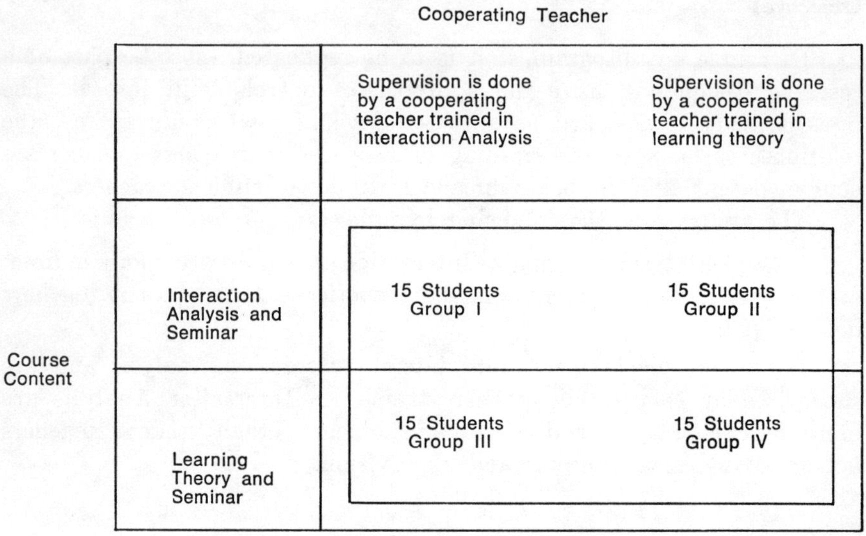

Figure 3. The Four Experimental Groups

Group II. Student teachers in this group are taught Interaction Analysis in a two hour a week lecture and a two hour a week laboratory. In addition, they have a two hour a week seminar with their college supervisor in which they can discuss problems they are having in their teaching. The cooperating teacher observes the student teacher formally once a week for 30 to 40 minutes, and spends one hour a week discussing the observation with the student.

Group III. Student teachers in this group are taught learning theory in a two hour a week lecture and a two hour a week laboratory. In addition, they have a two hour a week seminar with their college supervisor in which they can discuss problems they are having in their teaching. They are also observed formally for 30 to 40 minutes once a week by their cooperating teacher, who spends one hour a week discussing the observation with them. Although the cooperating teacher may use Interaction Analysis in his observation, he is clearly instructed not to discuss this tool or any of its terminology with the student teacher under any circumstances.

Group IV. Student teachers are taught learning theory in a two hour a week lecture and a two hour a week laboratory period. In addition, they have a two hour a week seminar with their college supervisor in which they can discuss problems they are having in their teaching. The cooperating teacher observes the student teacher formally once a week for 30 to 40 minutes, and spends one hour a week discussing this observation.

Research by Hough and Amidon (12), Zahn (16) and Kirk (13) indicates that twelve to thirty hours of training in Interaction Analysis affects the behavior and/or attitudes of student teachers. The present design which includes 105 hours of training in and application of Interaction Analysis therefore appears to be adequate.

Population and Sample

Approximately 60 student teachers will be involved in the experiment during each of five semesters, all of them participating in their second student teaching experience. The student teachers are assigned to experimental groups according to a randomized block design. Student teachers are assigned in equal numbers to the four conditions on the basis of the socioeconomic areas in which they do their student teaching, grade level taught and subject matter taught. One of the particular problems in the student teaching assignment at Temple University is the large number of placements in the "culturally deprived" areas of Philadelphia. By using this type of design, an attempt is made to control the influence on the results of this variable of the variable of differences in school settings.

The student teachers are all students in the Department of Secondary Education at Temple University. Nearly all of the students are residents of Philadelphia. Approximately fifty percent of the student teachers are girls. The four groups are compared on the basis of personality, attitudes, and college grades, in order to determine the influence of these variables.

Data and Instrumentation

Student teaching rating. Student teachers are rated at both the beginning and end of their student teaching experience by the same measuring instrument which the Department of Secondary Education normally uses to rate student teachers. Student teachers are rated by both their college supervisors and by impartial observers not involved in supervision. The impartial observers do not know which student teachers are in which of the four experimental groups.

Student teaching behavior. The Flanders System of Interaction Analysis is not only taught to student teachers, it is also used to assess changes in behavior that may take place over the semester. Each student teacher is observed for two hours at the beginning of the semester and for two hours at the end of the semester by a trained observer using the Flanders system. These observers are not the college supervisors and do not know which student teachers are in which of the four experimental groups.

Student teaching rating by pupils. The Student Perception of Teacher Influence Scale is used to assess the perception that the children have of their student teacher's behavior. The data are gathered on a nine point scale, and are analyzed statistically. This instrument was used initially by Amidon (2) and Anderson (4) with secondary school pupils, and has been adapted for use in the elementary school by Kirk (13). Both Amidon and Anderson report high reliability for this instrument.

Student teacher attitude. The Teaching Situation Reaction Test is used to assess student teacher attitudes. In general this test measures the student teacher's reaction to a classroom situation in terms of the direct-indirect dichotomy. A student teacher with a low score sees himself reacting fairly indirectly to a classroom situation, while a high score indicated a more direct reaction. Hough and Amidon (12) present information concerning the validity of the instrument. They found a split half reliability of .94 for the test. This test is given both at the beginning and end of the student teaching experience.

Student teacher personality. Rokeach's Dogmatism Scale is used to measure personality. A discussion of the test construct and validation procedure are available in Rokeach's *The Open and Closed Mind* (15). The aspect of personality measured by the test is the openness or closedness of a person's belief system.

Results and Conclusions

The results of the present study must be interpreted in the light of the early work which was done by Flanders and his associates.

Interaction Analysis was developed and refined by Flanders in the early 1950's. The early research on Interaction Analysis was designed to relate children's attitudes to patterns of teacher behavior. Flanders found that pupils of teachers who were observed to be indirect had more positive attitudes than pupils of teachers who were perceived by observers as being direct. These findings indicated that pupils of indirect teachers were more interested in subject matter and liked the methods used by their teachers better than did students of direct teachers (9: 10).

The results of this early research support the validity of Interaction Analysis as a procedure for predicting the general attitudes of children in a particular classroom.

The next research effort undertaken by Flanders and his associates was designed to determine the relationship between teacher behavior and student achievement. Several large studies were conducted both in a controlled laboratory setting and in normal classroom situations. All of these studies were carried out at the junior high school level and involved the teaching of social studies and mathematics.

In the first of these studies, Amidon and Flanders (2) found that dependent-prone eighth grade students who were taught geometry by indirect teaching methods learned more than dependent-prone children taught by direct methods.

In a large scale study, Flanders (9) isolated, for purposes of analysis, junior high school teachers whose pupils learned the most and the least after a two week experimental program in social studies or mathematics. Teachers of the higher achieving classes were found to differ from teachers of the lower achieving classes in the following ways: (a) they used five to six times as much acceptance of student ideas and encouragement of student ideas, (b) they used five to six times less direction and criticism of student behavior, (c) they talked ten percent less, and (d) they encouraged two to three times as much student-initiated talk.

Similar results to those found by Flanders between teachers of high achieving pupils and those of low achieving pupils were found by Amidon and Giammatteo when they compared 30 superior teachers with 150 randomly selected teachers in elementary schools. The 30 superior teachers were nominated by their supervisors and administrators (3).

Since all of this research appeared to have implications for teacher education, Flanders instituted an in-service program in which Interaction Analysis was taught as an observational tool. The in-service program was able to effect observable changes in teacher patterns of verbal behavior. In general, at the end of the experimental in-service program, these teachers evidenced more encouraging and accepting behavior and were less critical and more indirect than they had been at the beginning of the experiment (10).

Kirk conducted a study with student teachers in elementary education in which he taught Interaction Analysis to an experimental group and compared this group with student teachers who had no Interaction Analysis. He found that the experimental group talked less, had more pupil-initiated talk, and more often accepted pupil ideas than did student teachers in the control group (13). Zahn found that student teachers who learned Interaction Analysis developed more positive attitudes toward student teaching than did a control group of student teachers who were not taught Interaction Analysis (16).

Little, if any, systematic research has been done on the training of cooperating teachers to supervise student teachers. However, the recent work of Medley and Mitzel (14) and Zahn (16) does suggest that there is a relationship between the behavior and attitudes of co-operating teachers and growth in student teaching. While they found that the effect of the college supervisor on the student teacher was slight, the influence of the cooperating teacher and the classroom situation appeared to be great.

Much of the data from the present study is still not analyzed. However, the direction indicated by the early analysis is significant because of the consistency of the findings. When comparisons were made at the end of the semester between the student teachers who learned Interaction Analysis and those who did not, the following results were obtained:

1. Student teachers who knew Interaction Analysis talked less in the classroom than those who were trained in learning theory.

2. Student teachers who learned Interaction Analysis were more indirect in their use of motivating and controlling behaviors than those who were trained in learning theory.

3. Student teachers who were taught Interaction Analysis were more indirect in their overall interaction patterns than student teachers who were trained in learning theory.

4. Student teachers who were taught Interaction Analysis used more extended indirect influence than student teachers who were trained in learning theory.

5. Student teachers whose cooperating teachers learned Interaction Analysis used less extended direct influence than student teachers who were trained in learning theory.

6. Student teachers who were taught Interaction Analysis used less extended direct influence than student teachers who were trained in learning theory.

7. Student teachers who were taught Interaction Analysis used more extended acceptance of student ideas than student teachers who were trained in learning theory.

Perhaps the most significant implications of the early results of the continuing study are that they are consistent with, and support the previous work which has been done on the effect of Interaction Analysis on student teachers, as well as the earlier studies on the relationship between Interaction Analysis patterns and student attitudes and achievement.

In general, when student teachers are trained in Interaction Analysis they become more indirect, accept more student ideas, and criticize less than student teachers not so trained. Since Flanders found that teachers of children who had high achievement and positive attitudes were more indirect, accepted more student ideas, and used less criticism than teachers of children with low achievement and negative attitudes, there appears to be substantial evidence that the Interaction Analysis training is helping to produce teachers with appropriate teaching skills.

Implications

Perhaps the best estimate of the role of Interaction Analysis in the supervisory process is that it provides a basis for what might be termed the "self-directed supervisor." With Interaction Analysis the supervisor does not need to point to the teacher and give him directions for changing his behavior; the teacher can see this in the matrix. The teacher can observe himself, using a tape recorder and thus provide his own feedback without the presence of another person. While many teachers find the use of Interaction Analysis threatening at first, many also find it refreshing to be able to have objective data that they can study and thus make their own decisions about how they would like to change.

References

1. E. J. Amidon and N. A. Flanders. *The Role of the Teacher in the Classroom.* Minneapolis, Minnesota: Paul S. Amidon and Associates, 1963.

2. E. J. Amidon and N. A. Flanders. "The Effects of Direct and Indirect Teacher Influence on Dependent-Prone Students Learning Geometry." *Journal of Educational Psychology* 52: 286-91; 1961.

3. E. J. Amidon and M. Giammatteo. "The Verbal Behavior of Superior Teachers." Philadelphia: Group Dynamics Center, Temple University, 1964.

4. J. P. Anderson. "Student Perceptions of Teacher Influence." Unpublished Ph.D. thesis, University of Minnesota, 1960.

5. N. D. Bowers and R. S. Soar. "Studies of Human Relations in the Teaching Learning Process; V. Final Report; Evaluation of Laboratory Human Relations Training of Classroom Teachers." *Cooperative Research Project No. 469.* U. S. Office of Education, 1961. p. xii-210.

6. J. B. Conant. *The Education of American Teachers.* New York: McGraw-Hill Book Company, Inc., 1963.

7. J. H. Darwin. "Note on the Comparison of Several Realizations of a Markov Chain." *Biometrika* 46: 412-19; 1959.

8. H. A. Engle. "A Study of Openness as a Factor in Change." Unpublished Ph.D. thesis, Auburn University, 1961.

9. N. A. Flanders. "Teacher Influence-Pupil Attitudes and Achievement, Final Report." *Cooperative Research Project 397.* U. S. Office of Education, 1960.

10. N. A. Flanders. "Helping Teachers Change Their Behavior." University of Michigan, 1962.

11. N. A. Flanders and E. J. Amidon. "Two Approaches to the Teaching Process." *NEA Journal* 50 (5): 43-45; May 1962.

12. J. Hough and E. J. Amidon. "An Experiment in Preservice Teacher Education." Unpublished paper. American Educational Research Association, February 1964.

13. J. Kirk. "The Effects of Teaching the Minnesota System of Interaction Analysis on the Behavior of Student Teachers." Unpublished Ed.D. thesis, Temple University, 1964.

14. D. M. Medley and H. Mitzel. "Measured Changes in Student-Teaching Behavior." In: H. Schueler, M. Gold and H. Mitzel. *Improvement of Student Teaching.* Hunter College of the City University of New York; Project 730035, Educational Media Branch of the Office of Education, U. S. Department of Health, Education and Welfare.

15. M. Rokeach. *The Open and Closed Mind.* New York: Basic Books, Inc., 1960.

16. R. Zahn. "The Effect of Cooperating Teacher Attitudes on the Attitudes of Student Teachers." Unpublished paper. Glassboro State College, Glassboro, New Jersey, 1964.

Professional Integration and Clinical Research

Ted W. Ward

AS PROFESSIONAL educators in the second half of the twentieth century, we are uneasy in our sense of time. We feel an urgency to know, to understand, to solve, to innovate, to accomplish. And this should not be surprising. Our high-achieving society has identified education as the prime curator of its complex and chaotic problems. Caught in the revolution of "rising expectations," we examine the massive and diverse problems—increasing, changing and demanding as they are. And still unsure whether our tasks or our anxieties represent promise or threat, we accelerate our efforts, hoping that we are dealing with what may be the redeeming issues of our lives and world—all in a dynamic state of motion—all except time itself, that is, where there still remain only 24 hours in a day and 365 days in a year.

So population control, job training and retraining, mechanization, automation, impersonalization, social inequality, unemployability, urban decline and social chaos, clean air and pure water, and individual freedom and international assistance become problems looking to professional education for help. Yet in order to help solve these problems effectively, we must first seek solutions to our chronic problems within education.

We need, or so we are told, more research on educational issues, more planning by colleges and universities, more master planning by states, and better allocation of resources at the national level. Schools should be run more economically and universities should be more productive. They must be larger, yet not lose track of individuals. Educational research is to focus more on real problems and to carry the results through developmental stages to the point of service and action. And we must do this in the face of a severe drain on competent personnel.

New information must continue to grow in amount and availability. We are reminded of school dropouts and that we need superior instruction for superior students and better programs for the handicapped and disadvantaged. Teacher education programs must be expanded and improved as the teacher shortage increases again. So one could continue. Our literature is full of it: problems, problems, a few ideas—fewer solutions. At all levels, everywhere, there is to be better planning, more innovation, improved organization, greater efficiency—and education in the United States will be in good shape to solve the problems of our age.

Small wonder we have self-doubts and suffer anxious moments. Small wonder we are uneasy in our sense of time.

Lest the reader get the impression that I am building on pessimism, I warn him now of my optimism. I find the shift of responsibility to education in a real sense a triumph. Too long our society has failed to recognize that only a strong and vital educational system can give us handholds to a better future.

What is needed, however, is more than an acceptance and willingness to tackle some of these problems. And what is needed is more than inspiring statements and conventional exhortations about the magnitude of the problems and the need for vision and creative innovation. This is not to deny the necessity for creative solutions, for these are indeed urgently needed. Yet what is required, it seems to me, are explicit suggestions and descriptions about where and how we ought to direct ourselves so that we can maximize our effectiveness and minimize our inhibiting anxieties.

Where, then, might we turn for direction? What sort of creativity will be adequate to surmount the amalgam of challenges with power and vision?

We are reminded at every turn that scientific and technical knowledge has given us unprecedented opportunity to better understand, explain and predict the unknowns in our environment. Yet I fear that although we have new and more useful tools, these tools alone will not provide the creative solutions that are needed.

Gyorgy Kepes (6), Professor of Visual Design and Architecture at the Massachusetts Institute of Technology, has defined the problem well; as the artist among the scientists and as the prophet among the pragmatists, he writes:

Science has opened up immense new vistas, but we shrink from accepting the deeper and richer sense of life uniquely inherent in the new parameters of our twentieth-century world. Where our age falls short is in the harmonizing of our outer and our inner wealth. We lack the depth of feeling and the range of sensibility needed to retain the riches that science and techniques have brought within our grasp.[1]

He suggests that what is most needed are models that will "guide us to re-form our formless world." He identifies three aspects that contribute to the formlessness of our present life—our environmental chaos, our social chaos, and our inner chaos. He sets three basic tasks before us:

First of all we must build bridges between man and nature—construct a physical environment which is on a truly twentieth-century standard. Second, we must build bridges between man and man—create a new scale of social structure built from progressive common purposes. We must establish a sense of belonging, of interdependence, in order to achieve the teamwork that the first task demands. And, finally, we have to build bridges inside ourselves. Only if each individual can unify himself, so that one aspect of his life will not intercept and cancel another, can we hope to tackle the second task efficiently. . . .

The building of these bridges—the reintegration of all aspects of our life through twentieth-century knowledge and power—is our great contemporary challenge, and in this work the imaginative power of creative vision coupled with sensibilities can have a central role.[2]

Once again our plea for creative vision is heard. But here Professor Kepes goes beyond the conventional advice. He suggests a starting point. He suggests, and wisely so, that since we are seeking new visions of life, the artist possesses fundamental values which contribute to our visions:

. . . we respond to the images of artists because of their completeness; because their harmonies, rhythms, colors, and shapes touch us, and not just on one level or another of our being. . . . Art bids us touch and taste and hear and see the world. . . .

In its aspect of many-layered but unified experience, participation in a work of art often provides us with deep insight into the wholeness of the world.[3]

The other basic value that an authentic creative work of art offers to us is inherent in the proportion between its fundamental opposites: expressive vitality and formal order.

What makes a great painting far more than a well-ordered arrangement of colored surfaces, far more than an explosion of emotion, is its balanced proportioning of intense expression and disciplined structure.[4]

---

[1] Gyorgy Kepes. "Where Is Science Taking Us?" *Saturday Review,* March 5, 1966. p. 66. Reproduced from the Science and Humanity Supplement of *Saturday Review.*

[2] *Ibid.*

[3] *Ibid.*

[4] *Ibid,* p. 67.

How, you might ask, does this give us direction to our needed creative solutions? At what points is this advice relevant or how can it be transferred to educational problems?

Let me seek an answer by suggesting a means of incorporating the first value of the artist—completeness, wholeness. Perhaps there is a way of looking at the conglomerate of educational pursuits that will allow us to view it in its totality—a way of seeing our diverse concerns as part of a single community of thought and feeling.

To begin, we must get outside the confines of education and consider social enterprise at large. To see ourselves, and most important, to open our eyes to new viewpoints on ourselves in relation to other elements of our social order, we must occasionally back off; we must face up to the provincialisms which we have helped to build.

An Integrating View of Education

In modern society, every social enterprise which encompasses vocational activities is comprised of three essential components: practitioners, practitioner trainers, and researchers. These elements are introduced in Figure 1.

Figure 1. Elements of the Paradigm of Modern Social Enterprise

For sure, enterprises vary widely in terms of the degree of emphasis and the degree of development among the three components. In small business operations, for example, the practitioner (output worker) is almost a sole component, but not quite. In vocational schools, the function of trainer is in dominance. In consulting research organizations, the research component is predominant. Yet in each case, an elemental representation from all three components—practice, training, and research— can be identified. Typically in large corporations, business concerns, government agencies, even universities, the three components are well represented and fairly easy to distinguish.

The question of administration and supervision arises here. There is clearly a presence of administration and supervision in each of the components. These adjunct functions are assumed to exist in two relationships to each of the three components: (a) in the sense of overall administration and coordination *among* the three components, and (b) in the sense of enabling and monitoring acts *within* a given component.

Supervision, as an adjunct function, also presents another problem. In some enterprises, supervision is directly concerned with improvement of the operations and improvement of the personnel within the component, whether practitioners, trainers or researchers. In this sense, the supervision activity can be thought of as an extension of the training component, even when it operates apart from the identifiable, primary-training component. For example, the training component denoted when applying this paradigm to education is primarily the teacher education institution personnel. Yet inasmuch as school district supervisory personnel are often deeply involved in in-service training, the supervisory personnel are in one sense enhancers of the practitioner component and in another sense they are participants in the trainer component. By abstracting key elements and their relationships from a given situation, a paradigm facilitates communication about those aspects of the situation that are of interest. A paradigm loses its communication value if it tries to represent every aspect of a situation.

The basic problem of our paradigm is what to do with the supervisor—is he a part of the practitioner realm, part of the trainer realm, or a part of both? The resolution we make, for purposes of this paper, is reasonably functional. We see the school supervisor primarily as a functionary of the practitioner component, never forgetting, however, that he is most effective when operating as an extension of the training component. This resolution reduces ambiguity; nevertheless, it must be remembered that each of the three components has its own administrative and supervisory functionaries.

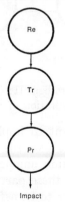

Figure 2. Paradigm I: Components in the
Configuration of a Nonprofessional Enterprise

Paradigm I (Figure 2) shows the three essential components in a relationship which exists typically in a nonprofessional enterprise. This relationship is characterized by a hierarchy of authority and a communication flow that is essentially one-way. Again, bear in mind that an administrative structure external to the three components ties them together to a focus on given tasks. For example, market research dictates what salesman training will seek to achieve in salesman (practitioner) activity. Salesman activity, in turn, achieves the sales objectives determined by management. Thus, management is the external binding force which commits all components to a given task to which the components make a ritualistic sequence of contributions.

In a professional field, these same three components exist, but they appear in a different configuration. They may not be more evenly balanced than in the nonprofessional enterprise, but there is a very important difference: in a well-developed profession, the communication flow is two-way and mutual. No component can insulate the other components from each other. Paradigm II (Figure 3) is a representation of the same three components but in a different configuration and tied together by additional communication lines.

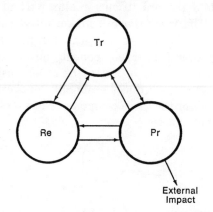

Figure 3. Paradigm II: Components in
the Configuration of a Profession

For sure, this is not meant to imply that the only distinguishing criteria of a profession are the patterns of communication and the absence of a hierarchy of dictation among the essential components, but only at this point to illustrate these particular differences and to pursue the differences to illustrate how to transform Paradigm I into Paradigm II.

We can think of education or any other social institution as a triad, a whole unit comprised of three components, each possessing specialities, commitments and vitality in its own right. A sense of unity is basic to wholeness.

Attaining a sense of unity alone is hardly adequate, however, and so we must examine the second value of the artist—a well-balanced proportion between expressive vitality and formal order. This second criterion for artistic expression is hardly visible in education at this point in time. I would also suggest that this task is the more crucial and also the most difficult to achieve.

Intense expression is now found within each of the three components of the educational enterprise; but formal order, vitally necessary to proportion, is lacking. The triad as a whole does not possess an organized life. Thus, the lack of a structured discipline hinders the search for creative solutions. These are reasons to believe that education has not yet become a profession. Further, there are clearly cases in education where the hierarchical linear flow and lack of inter-component feedback characterize our activities. It would be useful to consider what might happen if we were deliberately to add the missing communication links to our enterprise to achieve the status of Paradigm II. Hopefully, these communication links could develop from efforts to get the needed structure and, in turn, contribute to the maintenance of the structure. Figure 4 presents the two sets of communication additions which can be thought of as transformations implicit in changing Paradigm I to Paradigm II.

The concern for communication flow in the educational enterprise is not new. Many attempts have been made to conceptualize the com-

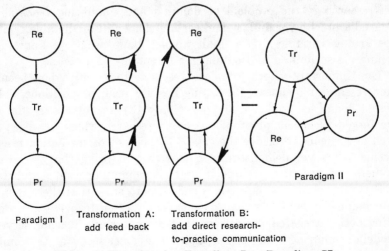

Figure 4. Transforming Paradigm I to Paradigm II

munication problem and various procedures to solve the problem have been employed. The procedures which are represented in Figure 4 as *Transformation A* have been reasonably successful. Very likely the relative success is attributable to the fact that the trainer-to-researcher (*Tr* to *Re*) communication feedback can be accomplished within the confines of a single institution, the university, and the practitioner-to-trainer (*Pr* to *Tr*) feedback can similarly be effected in the single domain created by the newer approaches to teacher education in which practitioners are regarded as essential partners in the internship operation. But *Transformation B* encounters much more resistance.

Numerous and commendable attempts to get the research component into interaction with the practitioner component have been made over the past quarter-century. Hardly a journal today fails to include a regular column, "From the Researchers." The American Educational Research Association is represented by the series, "What Research Says to the Teacher." Yet I can find little effort in the other direction: what the teacher says to researchers! Clearly the problem has not been solved by the tactic of restating research findings in simpler language. In a sense, language is the problem, but not in the senses of the lack of translation or of over-complexity.

The basic problem is far deeper: research is scientific inquiry and as such is concerned with careful description in a precisely meaningful vocabulary. Teaching practice is an area of human endeavor not yet well described in any precisely meaningful vocabulary. Thus, all attempts to get researchers and practitioners "together" are doomed to failure until research in the problem of defining and qualifying *teaching* has produced a precise vocabulary and certain elemental predictable relationships among variables. It is small wonder that "what we know about learning" is so limited and so difficult to employ in practice.

One important effort to relate research to practice has been the action research movement. Borrowing heavily from propositions of Kurt Lewin (7) and his students, Stephen Corey (3) and others in education have forged a concept of problem-solving research which has been promoted as a means to bridge the gap. Whether or not the action research movement has yet demonstrated a capacity to bring the work of researchers and practitioners into interactive communication is debatable. For the purpose of this paper, it is sufficient to state that there is inadequate empirical evidence that teachers are better teachers after completing action research projects or that a researching teacher serves as a model of inquiring behavior for pupils. The latter seems quite promising but awaits testing.

A more important observation for this paper is that action research quickly fell into disrepute among the researchers in education. Rather than bridging the gap, action research seems to have made it wider. Clearly the answer does not lie in having practitioners pretend to be researchers, nor does it lie in the opposite extreme of expecting researchers to take all the initiative in relating themselves to practitioner problems. Ernest Hilgard (5) reflects the bias of the researcher:

At any one time, scientists in experimental and theoretical fields can work only on the problems upon which they are prepared to work with the conceptual and material tools at hand. These may or may not be appropriate to the practical problem calling for solution.[5]

The research described later in the paper is to some degree a by-product of action research. We are translating even a larger application of Kurt Lewin's concept into education. Action research takes the position that better solutions to educational problems can be found through studies directed at the practitioners' decision-making tasks. Thus, we are developing studies which focus on practitioner behavior in such a way as to produce potent interaction with the training component and the basic research component of the professional triad. Because of the focus on the practitioner and his client-centered problems, we call these studies *clinical research*. Here we find a fundamental hope for creating meaningful interdependence among the components in the triad.

Intensive study of the practitioner's instructional tasks and instructional management problems designed to bring order to the profession is different from an "action research" concept wherein the goal is the getting of a transitory and highly pragmatic basis for an action decision. In clinical research, we apply the efforts of highly trained behavioral scientists to research *with* practitioners—first to develop descriptions of the real world in which their client-contact tasks exist, then to describe the variables the practitioners manipulate and the effects these manipulations produce, and finally, to so precisely define the vocabulary of the descriptions that corollary statements from basic research can be reliably identified and constructively related to applied problems.

This is not a new idea but attempts to actualize it have been rare. The current studies of instruction, as in the work of Bellack, Fattu, Flanders, Hughes, Smith, Taba, and Turner, to name a few, can be thought of as pioneering efforts in clinical research. The studies at Michigan State University are in this growing tradition, but we are making a somewhat different emphasis in that we see the clinical studies as but

[5] Ernest R. Hilgard. *Theories of Learning,* Second edition. New York: Appleton-Century-Crofts, Inc., 1956. p. 489.

a step in the process of more adequately relating the practitioner component to the research component, as well as to a vitalized teacher education component.

The old argument of basic research versus applied research is being put to rest by responsible behavioral scientists. Ernest Hilgard (5) helps to reduce the presumed dichotomy in the following statement:

Because scientists have to develop appropriate methods and concepts before their results can become efficient regulators of practice, their concerns for a time may appear to be remote from practical affairs, and some of their disputes will seem to be quibbles over distinctions that do not matter. All this suggests the need for patience and tolerance toward experimentation which pushes back the boundaries of the known and toward theory construction which attempts to sharpen the conceptual tools with which scientists can work.[6]

The activities subsumed in clinical research promise to help with the sharpening of conceptual tools to which Hilgard refers. It makes little sense to argue whether basic research is "better" or even "more useful" than applied research. Good research is good for certain reasons and these reasons are the same whether the problem is highly operational or abstract. Yet it is sensible to argue that research in any field will have impact on the practice of that field only to the extent that the field's real problems are known and adequately described.

Basic research is often plagued with the problem of external validity. Applied studies are inherently weak in internal validity. Clinical research offers a hope for resolving validity problems through careful matching of data from basic studies, as in laboratory conditions, and parallel data from field studies, where controls are less easy to maintain.

The focus on the clinical environment has proven to be productive of new data about practitioner behavior and much more. It has shown signs of enhancing all three of the communication loops in the paradigm. The clinical studies, largely because they are carried on in the practitioner environments in which the University is conducting teacher education operations, have demonstrably enhanced the practitioner-to-trainer *(Pr to Tr)* loop. Further, the practitioner-to-researcher *(Pr to Re)* loop has been affected by the data from the studies.

Our work began in 1963 as an outgrowth of conversation with a respected learning researcher. In the course of a discussion about the impasse between researchers and educational practice, he complained that although it was common enough for teacher educators to argue that teachers base their classroom activity on informal hypotheses or hunches about the learning variables, no one had ever taken the trouble either

[6] *Ibid.*

to substantiate the proposition or to identify and compile what hunches there might be.

Recognizing the validity of the complaint, we set about to test the proposition and to seek out the informal hypotheses on which a given set of elementary teachers were acting. Our practitioners are now providing data to the researchers, and in turn, the researchers are feeding back data which they glean from the outside research. So far, these efforts are confined to a process of checking the teaching hypotheses against the research literature in social psychology and human learning. The feedback consists of information about the existence or non-existence of relevant basic studies of the same matter, and where studies do exist whether or not they are mainly supportive or mainly refutative of the particular instructional hypothesis. Thus, the intensive focus on practitioner behavior has produced an enlarging ripple effect which is stimulating all three major communication loops. This is represented in Figure 5, where the concentric rings represent the increasing impact.

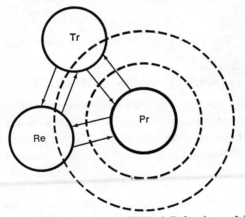

Figure 5. Impact of the Focus on Clinical Behaviors of Practitioners

But our concern is not just a matter of improving communications. What is being communicated is of vital importance. The need for form and order in education demands a concept of education as a unitary enterprise. Clearly the three components of the paradigm are held together by communication, but they are also mutually dependent—in that no one of the components makes much sense without the other two. Together they interact with the external world. Essential to the creation of form and order in human endeavor is the affixing of responsibilities. Thus, the paradigm can be elaborated to include a triangular exterior frame to represent the integrity or wholeness of the professional field and a set of input-output lines to indicate the major interactions of the system as a whole with the outside world. These lines are located in proximity to the components most directly responsible for the given external contacts.

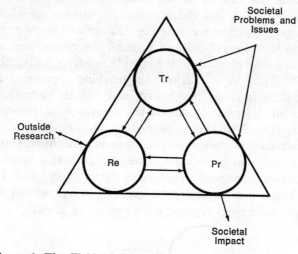

Figure 6. The Field of Education as an Interacting System

Clinical Studies as Research

Understanding the contributions and promise of clinical studies starts with a perception of clinical studies as research. Since such a perception must be built on specific illustrations, I will direct attention to the clinical studies with which I am most familiar—those which the Learning Systems Institute has designed and managed for Michigan State University's School of Teacher Education. This will highlight a number of the key elements of clinical research, particularly the following: (a) location of the data gathering in real instructional settings, (b) behavioral description of the teachers' activities within particular settings and in the course of striving for various learning objectives, (c) comparisons of data from several instructional settings in order to identify common elements and peculiar elements in sets of instructional behaviors, and (d) examination of behavioral descriptions (and the instructional hypotheses which they reflect) in the light of given bodies of outside research.

Observing Teaching

The clinical research studies to date have used decision making as the focal point for data gathering. The focus on decision making provides a means for "getting at" the various origins of the teaching behavior described. The series of studies the Institute has conducted since 1963 has refined a procedure for using the observer's judgment of an apparent decision-making function of the teacher as a focus for descriptive observation.

The studies in this series have served two purposes: (a) to derive instructional materials for preclinical teacher education courses; and (b) to provide descriptive data on the models of teaching which operate in our various clinical centers. The Focused Observation routine which has been developed for these studies uses observer data and self-report data from the teacher to investigate a particular act (as a product of some decision-making function) as it relates to: (a) what the teacher *sees* (perceives in the situation), (b) what he *knows* (information which he relates to the situation), and (c) what he *believes* (values which direct the particular action). Descriptions of the decisions teachers make in an instructional setting have been found to provide a useful focal point for behavioral description.

A second reason for the selection of decision making as the unit of behavior to be studied is that it allows a broad range of behaviors to be described. Rather than focusing on a limited facet, (e.g., the communicative interaction between teacher and students) activities of a wide and varied nature, even those which seem trite and perhaps inconsequential, can be taken into account. The following lists illustrate that the instructional function of the teacher, when viewed as an information system (9), involves behavior activities which require continuous decision making.

Input	*Processing*	*Output*
Watching	Selecting	Motivating
Listening	Planning	Managing
Reading	Evaluating	Leading
		Directing
		Coordinating
		Providing
		Telling.

Third, there is a practical advantage in studying small units of behavior, as is possible through the focus on decision making: the immense scope of teaching behaviors presents frustrations to those who would seek universal generalizations. The possibility of analyzing small samples of behavior and of generating partial models allows some useful products to be derived long before the completion of exhaustive descriptions of teacher behavior. In fact, it can be argued reasonably that exhaustive descriptions and universal statements here are impossible.

Still another reason for focus on the teacher decision making within the instructional context is that this allows for descriptions that can ultimately take into account the pragmatic method of decision theory as described by Bross (1). This method includes: (a) descriptions of a problem environment, (b) a set of actions, (c) a set of outcomes associated with the actions, (d) a set of probabilities associated with the outcomes of the actions, and (e) the desirability of the outcomes.

Finally, the focus on decision making as the unit of behavior has been found to provide an effective means to procure behavioral description of the small and discrete elements of which larger descriptions, even models representing "styles" of teaching, are composed.

In the particular Focused Observation procedure used most extensively so far, the descriptions include three basic segments: (a) *situation*—a description of the relevant elements in the immediate environment, (b) *action*—an account of the particular teacher behavior cited as an action based on an apparent decision, and (c) *consequence*—a description of the consequences of the action in terms of the immediate environment. After the observer writes these materials, the teacher is asked independently to verify what was seen and reported by the observer and to make any relevant additions he feels are important. In some cases, this interview is tape recorded. If there is fundamental disagreement between the observer and the teacher as to what occurred, the observation data are regarded as unreliable.

Both observer data and self-reported data are necessary. First, data that have been reported only by an observer or a teacher are less reliable than data obtained independently from both sources and then compared for consistency. Second, the adequate analysis of the situation and consequences usually depends upon data not available to the observer. In addition, the self-reported data and the way in which the teacher responds to inquiry are necessary in order to assess rationality.

Assessment of the rationality in teacher actions is one of the important problems in the present clinical studies. The Focused Observation procedure assumes that a degree of rationality exists in the sort of teacher action which the observer can describe as following relevant environmental cues. Indeed, much of the usefulness of the procedure is based upon the assumption that the instructional decision is a focal point revealing, in behavioral terms, what the teacher knows, sees and believes.

A diagram of the assumed relationship between a behavior and its roots is given in Figure 7.

Figure 7 illustrates the analysis problem: not all behavior is rooted in rational connections between what one knows, sees and believes. Before

A Teaching Behavior

Instructional
Decision:

A Focal Point for
Behavioral Description

What the Teacher Knows, Sees, Believes

Figure 7. Diagram of the Teacher's Instructional Decision as a Focal Point

other analyses can be made, it is necessary to make a distinction between what is and what is not rational behavior. Until we study the problem further, we are describing *rational* behavior as an action (or a deliberate non-action) preceded by thought which relates environmental cues to the selection of the action. Once rational decisions are identified, their roots can be traced. What the teacher has related to the problem can be investigated; this can be accomplished by inquiry into what he saw in the situation, what pertinent knowledge he related to the problem and what he believes to be worthy outcomes from the decision he made.

Compiling Models

In the clinical studies at Michigan State University, models of teacher behavior are constructed from the collected descriptions of teacher behavior. The term "model" has been associated with educational theorizing for more than a decade (2). Maccia (8) says that models fall into two categories: object model and characterization model. She discusses the two categories as follows:

Since there are objects and there are characterizations of them, the twofold distinction arises. If the characterization is about actually existing objects, then it is empirical. Our interest centers about empirical characterizations, for educational theorizing is an attempt to characterize actually existing objects falling within the domain of the educative process. In an empirical characterization, the statements not only express the nature of the objects, but also the way in which the objects are interrelated.[7]

Maccia also suggests that there are two uses for models:

In the first use, the object or characterization is a *model of* whatever is being represented; and in the second use, the object or characterization is a *model for*

[7] Elizabeth Steiner Maccia. "The Conceptions of Model in Educational Theorizing." *Occasional Paper 62-114 Cooperative Research Project 1632,* U.S. Department of Health, Education, and Welfare. Columbus, Ohio: Ohio State University Research Foundation. 1963. p. 47.

whatever it is represented in. A *model of* would be a representational model, while a *model for* would be a non-representational model.[8]

Using Maccia's definitions then, it can be said that the models derived in the clinical studies are empirical characterization models. They are intended, however, for both purposes—as models *of* teacher behavior (as in behavioral descriptions) and, after certain comparisons and modifications, as models *for* teacher behavior (as in theory building).

The particular set of teachers whose instructional behaviors are to be modeled are known as a "referent group." Such a group is convened to review the collection of some 200-250 descriptions of instructional decisions which were made in their own classrooms. They are asked to select those descriptions from the data pool which reflect behaviors they are presently encouraging in their interns. An arbitrary positive agreement level of 80 percent of the referent group is required on two questions in order to qualify a description for inclusion in the model being compiled. The two questions are: (a) Is the description adequate to provide a useful mental picture of the situation? and (b) Is the teacher action (or non-action) appropriate as you see "good teaching"? A third judgment concerns a rating of the representativeness of the occurrence of the described situation in classroom teaching at this level.

These three judgments are made independently by all members of a referent group. After those descriptions which are rejected by more than 20 percent of the group (on the first two questions) have been removed from consideration, the remainder are categorized and become the model for that group. The referent group is asked, as a final step, to arrive at an acceptable statement of an operating hypothesis which adequately expresses the basis for each behavior in the model.

After final editing and hypothesis verification, the result is a collection of about 125 to 200 behavioral descriptions, organized in terms of the particular instructional problem to which each description relates.

Comparisons Among Models

One of the more immediately interesting outcomes of these studies is the capability of comparing models of instructional behavior as it exists in differing situations. Our analyses of such comparisons are just beginning now, and, as yet, there are no data to report. We have under way a study of highly competent "center-city" elementary teachers in Detroit, Grand Rapids, and Flint. The descriptions in the model from this referent group are to be compared with the models derived from three other

[8] *Ibid.,* p. 48-49.

groups of outstanding elementary teachers (whose teaching assignments are not in "center-city"). Thus, we hope to get some clues about any behavioral differences which may distinguish the successful teachers in the urban center from the successful teachers in more ordinary locations.

The analysis procedure consists of: (a) inspecting two or three models to identify behaviors which are common to both, and which are peculiar to each; (b) verifying the inspections by reconvening the referent groups to consider whether behaviors which are not found in their respective models are a result of chance or of real exclusion; (c) adding into each model those descriptions which each referent group agrees also properly belong within their behavior model; and (d) re-inspecting the models for common and peculiar behaviors.

The procedure can be described as a comparison of intersecting sets where the identification of elements common to two sets must take into account the likelihood that elements which appear to be exclusive in one set may be a product of chance. A generalized paradigm (Figure 8) illustrates the procedure:

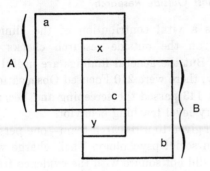

A and B: Two sets of behavioral descriptions

a: Behaviors peculiar to A set

b: Behaviors peculiar to B set

c: Behaviors common to both sets

x: Common behaviors which were *collected* only in A data

y: Common behaviors which were *collected* only in B data

Figure 8. Paradigm Illustrating the Comparison of Sets of Behavior Samples in Two Models

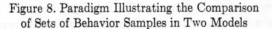

The fruitfulness of this kind of comparison activity will enable us to determine the usefulness of model derivation as a research tool. At the same time, it provides for increased focus and relevance of selection of training experiences as we prepare teachers for the particular tasks toward which they are aspiring.

Other comparisons that can be made in further studies would include:

1. Models of teacher behavior derived from middle-class neighbor-

hoods compared with those derived from culturally-deprived neighborhoods

2. Statements about teacher role and behavior which students encounter in preclinical coursework in education compared with models encountered in field experiences

3. Models of teacher behavior in elementary teaching compared with models of secondary teaching

4. Models of teacher behavior in selected fields of special education teaching compared with models of elementary and secondary teaching

5. Comparisons of models of behavior operating in various secondary school subjects

6. Models based on different concepts of "good" and "bad" teaching.

At present, we lack precise definitions upon which to base the crucial distinction between "general" and "special" in educational methods; much confusion in teacher education and in teacher evaluation can be traced to this lack.

Checking Instructional Behavior Against Outside Research

Although we see this step as a vital contribution of the clinical studies, to date we have only run the outside research checks on one set of behavioral descriptions. But the general findings are useful to report here. In the particular study, there were 210 Focused Observations in the starting data pool. Of these, 143 passed the screening and became elements in the model of elementary level teaching behavior.

The 143 descriptions were then given to a research team—one person in learning and the other person in social psychology. Their charge was to note any teacher decision which did not square with the evidence from research. They had no power to delete—only to challenge—since it was possible that they might be wrong about the classroom application of evidence from laboratory sources. Their obligation after challenging a teacher decision was to write a critique in which they reviewed the research which suggests a particular change in the operating hypothesis. They also had to suggest an alternative behavior which would be more in agreement with research. Of the 143 decisions, only four were challenged by the researchers. Perhaps more significant was their observation that specific research evidence spoke to less than half of the behaviors described. Thus, we have demonstrated, at least in this set of samples, that teaching is not wildly out of harmony with the basic research that can be meaningfully related to the teaching tasks.

Summary of the Research Contributions of the Clinical Studies

There are three groups of outcomes toward which our clinical studies have been moving. The first group is concerned with refined procedural techniques for documenting, analyzing and compiling teacher behavior samples. The second group accompanies the first as a contribution to educational theory: a set of statements concerning the function of general and special behaviors as they can be shown to relate to particular elements of environment or learner characteristics. The third class of outcomes is the most promising: the merger of data from behavioral studies in education with precise outcome statements from outside research. This may prove to be a useful new approach to bridging the gap between research and practice in education, first, in the sense of more adequate use of outside research by the education profession and, second, in the sense of stimulating research which will focus more adequately on basic problems of educational practice.

Relating Clinical Research to Teacher Education

Behavioral science is coming of age, and we are recognizing that a well-ordered educational profession will be based upon behavioral science approaches. Behavioral research in the problems of human learning and in the practice of instruction is a rapidly expanding field. Clinical studies of learning and teaching are carried on as a fundamental part of the environment in which teachers receive their practical training; thus, they afford an added dimension for the training experience itself. Since clinical research is less threatening to practitioners than abstract and remote laboratory research, trainees and supervisors are able to comprehend and utilize the findings. Further, they are more able to contribute and recognize the value of their contributions. Clinical research is concerned with the very problems which practitioners identify; furthermore, it begins with descriptions in the real environments, not just in the highly controlled and contrived environments of the laboratory. Like teaching itself, clinical research faces up to the ever-present problem of complexity— solutions are rarely generalizable without many provisions about the wide array of confounding variables.

Clinical research uses an essentially positive orientation. Studies of teaching implicitly acknowledge that what experience has taught practitioners is worth knowing. There is plenty that is right about teaching today; plenty to build upon. Alert practitioners who grow along with the demands of their duties are a powerful resource. We do well to build teacher education programs upon the models of excellent teaching which exist in a large number of public school classrooms.

Yet we have much to learn in order to be able to improve preservice and in-service education and to make supervision more effective. We do not even have highly developed data sources about needed change. In the absence of better data, we can treat the complaints which constitute the day-to-day counseling problems as informal feedback. This source is readily available. I have noted two major criticisms of the preclinical courses: lack of reality and lack of definiteness.

The student often tells us that his preclinical courses lack a sense of immediacy and reality. He wonders if what he is expected to learn is really giving him a true picture of teaching. He seems unconvinced that there is anything he can learn in these courses which will make much difference in his future as a teacher. And he hears other people, even respected professors and school teachers, who reinforce his suspicion. He begins to suspect that there are people in the teacher education program who have been passed over by progress—people whose concepts about what teaching is all about, what the schools are like, and what children are like, are concepts from yesterday.

And we have to wonder about relevance. Do our students learn the knowledge and skills they will actually need? How well does the teacher education program agree with what the student finds when he gets into his own first teaching position? We like to believe that colleges which provide much of the teacher education experience right in the real environment of the public school are less prone to this criticism. Yet, we still hear the criticism that what comes before the student teaching or internship has little apparent relationship to the demands of real classroom teaching. Many students report that the pre-student teaching work does not have the kind of relevance that would make the most sense. Some find that teaching does not look like they thought it would look. Part of this problem is related to the fact that a student has a notion of teaching largely produced by his own past experience as a learner through long years of elementary, secondary and college education. We lack imaginative ways to help him make the shift from student to teacher.

The lack of definiteness is even more difficult to cope with. Experienced teachers know full well that few magic formulas exist. Teaching requires a quick-thinking, imaginative response to a kaleidoscopic array of problems and needs. There is truth in our complaint that every situation is different. So we might want to shrug off the criticism of fuzziness in teacher education—we are tempted to argue that it must be indefinite and vague. To get any workable solutions to the vagueness problem, research must be called in. Few careful studies of the behaviors of competent teaching exist. There has been a steady flow of interesting research on teacher attitudes, teacher personality, and other psychological investigations of teachers and learners; but descriptive pictures of what good teachers *do* in particular settings are scarce.

Clinical studies can fill this void. For sure, attitudes and personalities are important, but basic traits and personality attributes are almost hopelessly resistant to improvement efforts. On the other hand, role perceptions do shift, behavior styles and actions are picked up from the models which exist in training or employment. It is especially clear that the supervising teacher in the student teaching experience is a powerful behavior model. We need descriptive research in order to get a better picture of what these behavior models look like; this will be the basis for developing materials and experiences in the preclinical phases of teacher education which will communicate these models more rapidly to the teacher-in-training. We expect this approach to provide a definiteness which seems now to be lacking. Teacher education can become a set of experiences which enable the student to begin to operate within the framework of the best teaching models available in real practice.

Models of teaching exist now, and certainly their impact is communicated—imprinted—on newcomers to teaching. Yet most models are largely implicit and their communication is now unsystematic. If the presently operating implicit models of teacher behavior could be made explicit, this would allow for more orderly approaches in teacher education, since the objectives of teacher behavior would be more visible and more susceptible to evaluation. When the components and objectives of teacher behavior are made more visible, the design of preclinical experiences can be more consistent with clinical experiences. Systematic revision can be initiated to experimentally modify teacher behaviors which are found to be inconsistent with outside evidence.

High-Efficiency Training Devices

Development of high-efficiency training materials and devices in teacher education awaits an adequate base of behavioral research of educational practice. Outstanding use of training-problem simulators and other high-efficiency training devices has been made in several fields, notably aviation, navigation, and space science. It is significant that the fields most ready and able to develop high-efficiency training procedures are those fields already characterized by a high degree of behavioral research on practitioner tasks.

An outgrowth of the Michigan State University clinical studies is a project in simulator technology for teacher education. In the development of our first instructional problem simulator, we have reduced teacher behavior to one common behavioral element: instructional decision making. And now we are inventing ways to confront students with small-scale instructional decisions, in order to give them practice in thinking as a teacher must.

We hypothesize that if the student can learn to seek and select environmental data and to base his instructional decisions on the important characteristics of the problem situation, he will develop a versatile and useful teaching skill. He will begin to adopt a systematic habit of using observations about what *is* in planning his teaching moves and evaluating the outcomes of his actions. Thus, he can profit from success *and* failure. Exciting possibilities are opened up to us once we commit ourselves to a crisp definition of the basic behaviors we want in professional practice.

Methodology as Hypotheses

In order to use high-efficiency methods, learning tasks must be highly specified. A behavioral theory of teaching can generate suitable specifics. It is useful to think of the teacher as a data processor—receiving from the immediate environment information which is to be processed within the framework of the stored data about objectives, procedural intentions, content to be communicated, and so forth. It is reasonable to suggest that teaching the rudiments of this particular behavioral style is preferable to a teacher education which attempts to teach "principles of learning" and a methodology which students perceive as precepts.

Despite pedagogical claims that there are general principles which operate in practice, these principles remain largely untested precepts, rarely being systematically treated as hypotheses needing empirical testing and subsequent revision. Most of these so-called principles are rooted in valid psychological experimentation or sound sociological observation. The difficulty, however, seems to be related to the craving we pedagogues have for generating larger and larger statements; what begins as a small-scale generalization from careful data soon is passed on to a whole generation of teachers as a large-scale principle of learning.

Indeed, precepts and generalizations can blind us to reality. No wonder our alert students rebel when they find that what they have learned simply does not work. Failure is interpreted as fallacy in the precept or, worse yet, inadequacy in the person. How much more secure and able to grow is the teacher who sees methodology as hypotheses!

We need to get closer to data and stay there. We need to develop in teachers not so much a knowledge of all there is to know about learning, for this is clearly impossible, but a systematic habit of basing instructional decisions upon whatever relevant data is available in the immediate environment of the classroom. Methodology can be thought of as a process in which the teacher (a) seeks cues by observing the dynamics of the classroom moment, (b) combines these cues with the aspirations and objectives he has for the learners (using his own hypothesis about learning), (c) makes a "move," and (d) evaluates the consequences of the move and the hypothesis on which he acted, in order to be able to make a better prediction next time.

Complicated though this may sound in verbal description, the human mind is capable of carrying on far more difficult cyclical processes than this one. Development of the habits of making appropriate observations, diagnoses, predictions and evaluations must be a major objective of professional education. Once established, such mental routines provide a highly flexible format for the teacher as he enters a career loaded with new and unpredictable demands.

Getting Started in Clinical Research

One of the first steps in building the Michigan State University clinical studies was the design of a basic data-gathering procedure particularly suited to the opportunities for observation and discussion presented within the social structures of the clinical and preclinical courses in teacher education. This first procedure, which has been through five basic revisions and now is widely used in two different forms, has the capability of generating descriptions of teacher actions in terms of the environmental cues and the cognitive processes of the teacher. The procedure uses observer data plus self-reported data by the teacher; the self-reported data is obtained without subjective clues and thus constitutes a basis for reliability tests of the observer's data. One form of the procedure uses tape recordings and time measurements of response latencies to produce additional data about the degree of rationality in the teacher's decisions.

When the Focused Observation procedure was developed by Southworth, Hoffman and Ward, it was hoped that other behavioral research data-gathering procedures could be as skillfully tailored to the peculiar opportunities in student teaching and internship operations. It was intended that, in time, a battery of behavioral study techniques could be borrowed, transformed and created for use in the large field of study available within teacher education.

In the past two years, we have made many observations and have come to some conclusions which can now serve as guidelines for clinical research instrument development. These we are recommending for use by our various coordinators and consultants who are interested in improving our arsenal of research instruments.

1. *The necessity of focus.* The first suggested guideline is that a behavioral study instrument suitable for research on instruction must have a precise focus. Case-study approaches in which everything available is gathered and diagnosed tend to diffuse the data and seriously inhibit meaningful analysis. A focus gives rudimentary delimitation and serves to avoid the classical problem of gathering more data than has value.

In the Focused Observation, for example, the observer uses the moment of teacher action as the focal point between the environmental data and the teacher perceptions, aspirations, objectives, knowledge and beliefs which affect the decision. Thus, the decision moment is a focus—there is something to look for, something to describe and something to discuss with the person observed. Each of the several instructional behavior studies which have come to national attention has such a focus. Developers of instruments for studying other aspects of practitioner behavior can get useful ideas about how to get suitable focus from these studies.

2. *The demand for range.* We have established that focused procedures can also have range. Research on instructional behavior is still a fairly primitive undertaking; we cannot afford premature judgments about which elements of behavior are important and which are unimportant. A common pitfall is to develop procedures which tap some area, some particular element which is logically relevant to instructional competence, and to place all subsequent effort on this area.

Perhaps it is more academically respectable to do one thing very thoroughly than to do several things only fairly well, but a danger lies in the tendency to inflate the relative importance of whatever has been selected to be done. Until empirical evidence is available about the relative importance (for particular kinds of instructional problems) among verbal interaction, question-asking strategies, patterns of instructional "moves," classroom climate, and so forth, a very broad range of investigation is needed. Building up empirical evidence that one of these classes of variables is indeed germane to instructional competence and learning achievement is an intermediate stage. To some degree, the Flanders (4) interaction analysis studies have established evidence for the importance of verbal interaction vis-à-vis classroom climate. Now is the time to correlate these studies with studies of other sets of variables in the instructional environment.

3. *The need for self-report data from the practitioner.* Any observation procedure that attempts to get a meaningful picture of what is going on in an instructional or management situation must take data from the practitioner. In the classroom, for example, the only person able to identify what particular elements of past experiences and case histories, what objectives, what environmental cues and what personal biases were operating in a given behavioral sequence is the teacher. The observer can note the actions and, to some extent, the perceptible interactions, but analysis must get behind these notations—ideally must get into the mind of the practitioner. Clearly, what the teacher knows about the basis of his action must be investigated; clearly, he should be given a role in the data gathering.

4. *Minimizing observer judgments.* Reliability, particularly inter-observer reliability, is largely dependent on the extent of observer judgment required. Even straightforward objective reporting is hard to keep free of judgments and other value decisions, but the behavioral research techniques which prove to be the most unmanageable and the most demanding of rigorous, costly training and monitoring are those in which the data gatherer is asked to be a reporter and a judge simultaneously. Reliability drops when he must categorize or qualify during the observation or interview. Developers of instruments for clinical research should pay close attention to this problem.

5. *Data gathering as educational experience.* One of the promising values of clinical research is the design and use of data-gathering procedures wherein the persons assigned to gather data are engaging in experiences which have educational value for them. Since clinical research is conceived as an adjunct of training programs within the field environments of education, such data-gathering procedures can open up a fairly large and economical set of data sources. Thousands of people at any given moment are engaged as trainees and supervisors in practicum experiences within the educational training field. These people are spending much time observing, their attention may or may not be focused on important variables; they will usually talk with the people they have been observing, they may or may not talk about anything important. We have found that with a reasonable amount of structure these people can be gathering data of broader significance while engaging in more valuable observations and dialogues. This guideline leads toward meaningful data-gathering tasks (essentially describing and asking) rather than non-meaningful tasks (such as tallying or sorting).

A discussion of what we have learned would be incomplete without a word about the inadequacies we have noted in our work. It was our hope that the Focused Observation technique would provide a way to investigate a wide range of instructional variables with a minimum of predisposition to exclude any potentially important variable. The focus on decision-making moments has provided a very workable "handle" to get hold of the dynamic variables. We can build highly meaningful pictures of teaching in any kind of setting and in an efficient manner. Analyses of these data do get behind the overt acts into the minds of teachers. Comparisons of sets of described behaviors do put the finger on certain kinds of differences in various settings.

The derived materials have been found to be useful in preclinical teacher education courses and for the development of simulator sequences. Yet we are not getting at everything—far from it. Our derived models are like vignettes. The connective tissue is weak. The threads that tie instructional moments into instructional sequences still elude us. It is as if we have the concrete blocks which build the wall, but we cannot find the mortar. We are opening new investigative avenues, building new observational techniques on the guidelines already cited, hoping to delineate more adequately patterns, sequences and "moves" in the instructional task. To develop our approaches, we are incorporating ideas from the work of others whose approaches to research on teaching have been different.

In summary, teaching is an art, yet it need not be purely intuitive. Learning is affected by philosophical, physiological, psychological and sociological factors; and since these can be studied through orderly processes, it follows that scientific inquiry can help us toward an orderly comprehension of learning and teaching.

Kepes (6) inspires us to seek models that will re-form a formless world: creative vision flows from a balance of the two crucial values— expressive vitality and formal order. Formal order requires theory; the least inhibiting sort of theory is theory which assists in comprehension of the essence of the art. A creativity without theory is purely intuitive and cannot be taught.

In the study of teaching, we must build behavioral theory. Practitioner description must account for activity more than for static traits, more for *doing* than for being. The clinical research we have been describing is leading into such theory building. At this time, six rudimentary statements comprise the assumptions in the behavioral theory of teaching which is emerging. These statements can be seen as extensions of previous assumptions in educational theory, as in Ryans (10), who implies that (a) teacher behavior is a function of situational factors, and (b) teacher behavior is observable.

1. (a) Teaching is a process in which one person's behavior affects another's behavior in such a way as to induce change.

(b) Teaching is a generalized set of behaviors which can be examined and explained in terms of a general theory of human behavior.

2. Teacher behavior is the singular mode of expressing the composite of beliefs, knowledge, attitudes, perceptions and aspirations which constitute teaching in any given situation.

3. Teacher behavior can be viewed as being comprised of (a) rational acts and (b) nonrational acts.

4. (a) The rational acts of teaching can be identified as having origin in rational decision-making processes.

(b) The nonrational acts of teaching can be identified in terms of their lack of basis in rational decision-making processes.

5. Teaching behavior can be described as a set of acts made as more or less rational responses to environmental (situational) factors.

6. Meaningful descriptions of teaching behavior relate environmental factors, teaching acts, and behavioral outcomes.

Such theory should provide a framework that is useful in numerous contexts. As Hilgard (5) states: "Theories serve more than one purpose: they attempt to organize existing knowledge, they attempt to provide threads or hypotheses toward new knowledge, and they may also furnish principles by which what is known can be used." [9] We can observe the power of the behavioral theory of teaching by examining the empirical evidence obtained from the clinical research, the questions it answers, the purposes it serves, and the new questions it raises.

Behavioral theory can help us see ways to integrate our enterprise into a set of communicating components, professionally bound together in mutual dependencies. Clearly, the science of human behavior undergirds the practitioner arts in education. Art and science must be reconciled—expressive vitality and formal order must be balanced. Kepes (6) summarizes the hope and implies a challenge:

Only complete acceptance of the world which is being born can make our lives genuinely acceptable. Such acceptance implies, above all, two concrete tasks. One, in every field of human endeavor we must advance to the furthest frontiers of knowledge possible today. Two, we must combine and intercommunicate all such knowledge so that we may gain the sense of *structure,* the power to *see,* in the deepest, richest sense, our world as an interconnected whole.[10]

[9] Hilgard, *op. cit.,* p. 485.

[10] Kepes, *op. cit.*

Response to this challenge can lead to an integrated and dynamic profession.

References

1. I. Bross. *Design for Decision.* New York: Macmillan Company, 1953.

2. A. P. Coladarci and J. W. Getzels. *The Use of Theory in Educational Administration.* Stanford: Stanford University Press. 1955.

3. S. M. Cory. *Action Research Ti Improve School Practices.* New York: Teachers College, Columbia University, 1953.

4 N. Flanders. *Teachers Influence, Pupil Attitudes and Achievement.* Comparative Research Project No. 397, Minneapolis: University of Minnesota, 1960.

5. E. R. Hilgard. *Theories of Learning,* Second edition. New York: Appleton-Century-Crofts, Inc., 1956. p. 485-90.

6. G. Kepes. "Where Is Science Taking Us?" *Saturday Review,* March 5, 1966.

7. K. Lewin. *Resolving Social Conflicts.* New York: Harper & Brothers, 1948.

8. Elizabeth Steiner Maccia. "The Conceptions of Model in Educational Theorizing." *Occasional Paper 62-114 Cooperative Research Project 1632,* U. S. Department of Health, Education, and Welfare. Columbus, Ohio: Ohio State University Research Foundation, 1963.

9. D. G. Ryans. "Teacher Behavior Theory and Research: Implications for Teacher Education." *Journal of Teacher Education* 14:274-93; September 1963.

10. D. G. Ryans. *Characteristics of Teachers.* Washington, D.C.: American Council on Education, 1960.

Strategies for Instructional Change:
Promising Ideas and Perplexing Problems

Ben M. Harris

THIS paper will attempt to develop only four ideas. I think these ideas are important, although others may be more so. These ideas seem especially important to me if our concern truly is for the supervisor as an agent of change in teacher learning, and if we are concerned with research and the improved practice of supervision for instructional improvement.

My four ideas in overview can be stated as follows:

1. Research into supervisor behavior and especially as exhibited in in-service education and curriculum development is a critical need. We need more, better, new kinds, and a greater variety of research in this field of specialization.

2. Theoretical models and concepts are available to supervisors and researchers for use in designing both research studies and supervision programs. These models or concepts can be borrowed from a variety of behavioral sciences and adapted to the specific conditions of the school operation.

3. Promising new or remodeled practices have been developed in considerable variety. These need field testing and evaluation in more systematically designed programs.

4. The development of improved supervisory program models is of critical importance. The excessive pressures for instructional change of present and future years demand more highly developed programs and strategies, in the hands of more knowledgeable supervisors, with greater resources at their disposal.

The Need for Research

Many needs for educational research are being recognized. Supervision research seems about to be included. I aired some of my views on this point in an article for *Educational Leadership* in 1963 (10). Here I will concern myself only with a few points. Some problems of the past, the need for descriptive studies of supervisory behavior, and two other researchable areas will be mentioned.

Research Problems

It is one thing to say we need more and better research; it is quite another problem to offer guidelines for such efforts. Most readers are fully aware of the studies completed in recent years as they relate to instructional supervision. The studies directly focusing upon supervisory practice have been very few in number and largely from doctoral dissertations. A wonderful flurry of research activity has been reported in the past few years by Flanders, Hughes, Ryans and others on teacher characteristics, classroom behavior, and observation analysis. These studies have extended our knowledge of teacher behavior, raised new questions about the teaching-learning process, and sharpened some tools for research and supervision beyond the previous work of Medley and Mitzel (23) some years earlier.

Notable indeed is the lack of research on the supervisor and supervisory programs and practices in education. We continue to emphasize studies in this field which deal with teacher opinions of supervisors, principals' opinions, contrasting perception of roles, and role conflicts. These studies have been valuable, but it is time to change focus and to sharpen it too. Neither the quality nor the significance of these studies warrants much more replication.

The limited significant research directly related to supervisory behavior is especially notable when we consider research in the field of educational administration. While not extensive, this field has been much more actively concerned with research, and many studies in administration have been focused upon administrative behavior. The Ohio Leadership Studies (29), the Descriptive Characteristics Study (14a) project on the behavior of the elementary school principal, and various studies of role perceptions by Gross and others illustrate administrative research which leaves the field of research in instructional supervision in a distinctly inferior position.

It may well be that research in supervisory behavior might be accelerated and improved substantially in the years immediately ahead by modified replications of some studies in educational administration. I do not suggest this as an ideal or exclusive approach. But the many similarities in practices and purposes of practitioners in these fields offer some promise for such research endeavors.

The recent study of administrators and the adoption of innovations by Carlson (6) might well be redesigned and repeated with supervisors as the focus. The school simulation materials developed for the Descriptive Characteristics Study project are available and might provide a relatively simple approach to the study of supervisory behavior patterns.

Further suggestions for studies building upon or adapted from other research efforts could be described. Let me hasten to add, however, that research of quite different kinds should not be neglected. Many aspects of supervisory behavior are very different from administrative behavior. These aspects need attention too!

Exploratory and Descriptive Needs

One of the serious bottlenecks to improving supervisory practices derives from a very simple array of facts. The work of supervisors is characterized by very diverse human relationships, a multiplicity of kinds of tasks, and no fixed locus of operation. The supervisor works in many organizational climates, deals extensively with subordinates, peers, and superordinates, ranges over a wide variety of substantive and procedural problems, produces no readily visible product, is held only vaguely accountable for certain on-going events in the school, and is almost immune to systematic evaluation. This is not a value judgment. It is an objective attempt to generalize in describing supervisory realities in our schools. To a lesser degree, these same things could be said of teachers and principals, but these are striking characteristics of supervisors and apply only in a limited way to the other two professional groups.

The problems offered to researchers in understanding human behavior are extremely complex at best. With respect to supervisory behavior, the problems grow and multiply because of the complexity of the job, the variety of relationships involved, and the transiency of the operation itself. This problem calls for elaborate descriptive studies which have not yet been attempted. My feeble efforts at describing supervisory staffs and responsibilities in five school districts served largely to illuminate the difficulties involved. Most studies of supervisory behavior look at the supervisor as an isolated person or the supervisor as a homogeneous class of professionals, and both views are terribly unrealistic.

Resistance to Change

That resistance to change is a problem hardly needs elaboration. Its causes and treatments need exacting study, however, and this does justify some emphasis.

Brickell's (4) studies have highlighted the well known facts about the administrator as an obstacle to change. Carlson's (6) studies have provided new insights about administrators who do and those who do not promote change.

A whole host of unanswered questions remain in relation to this problem of resistance to change. The dynamics of the role of the principal and superintendent as stabilizers and resistors are only vaguely understood. Supervisors in central staff, state agency, intermediate unit, and federal government positions have rarely functioned as agents of change. This paradox cries for analysis. Studies by Gross, Hunter (17), Kimbrough and Seigel are among many which suggest vital relationships between community power structure and school programs.

Lazarsfeld's (20) analysis of the effects of Congressional investigations upon the social science curricula and teachers is a classic example of the need for studies of external influence on instructional practices at various levels. It would be naive, indeed, to believe that events of the past decade emphasizing changes in physical science, abstract mathematics, foreign languages, and English, while virtually ignoring applied mathematics, sociology, comparative religion, consumer economics, political science, and intercultural education were dictated by Sputnik or by chance. Economic, social and political forces operate at all levels to influence the curricula and instructional practices which supervisors can promote. The dynamic operation of these forces upon the teacher and supervisor working at local levels needs much objective study.

Supervisory Practices

Specialization of function is a growing characteristic of educational programs. Sometimes we wonder about the pupil getting lost in this process of increasing specialization. Yet certainly instructional supervision is a specialty distinct from management and teaching functions. Supervision is emerging as a true profession and increasing specialization of practices seems inevitable. Supervisors cannot continue in servant roles and expect to be effective as change agents. Considerable attention needs to be given to supervisory practice in terms of external and internal relationships. Attention to supervisory practice has focused in the past on relations with teachers, principals and students. Few studies of supervisor-supervisor relationships exist. Similarly, comparative studies of supervisory programs employing various combinations of practices are rarely found.

Even when we look at supervisory programs of rather simple design, systematic evaluation is rarely built-in. As a result, most of what we now employ as "tools of the trade" gain their validity, if any, from crude estimates. We rely heavily upon assumption and hope to guide supervisory practices. A few basic activities have been researched by scholars in other disciplines. Rogers' (25) studies of nondirective interview techniques, studies of lectures vs. group discussions (21; 15), and a number of studies of role playing (19) and brainstorming (7) illustrate the contributions of behavioral scientists to instructional supervision.

An urgent need of this immediate period in which instructional change is demanded on all fronts is a revolution in supervisory practice. This will demand extensive field testing of a great variety of known practices to establish more clearly the unique and the common values of each. Without this, large strategies and designs for instructional change are not likely to emerge.

The use of raw power and indoctrination to secure changes in instructional practice has its advocates and recent examples of this abound (in state and national curriculum studies, for instance). There appears to be a tendency for these changes to be superficial rather than fundamental, and temporary rather than permanent. Furthermore, the abundance of undesirable side-effects derived from changes brought about under such conditions leaves much to be desired. It might be, that the so-called "new" or "modern" mathematics being introduced in elementary schools will not be desirable after all, if teachers learn to go through a sequence of "teacher-proof" procedures and to abdicate responsibility for teaching.

A number of studies do illustrate possible directions for further research and practice. DeVault's efforts to improve elementary mathematics teaching by alternate in-service education strategies demonstrated the importance of the consultant in connection with the use of mass media. A study we are now completing seems promising as a test of the effectiveness of televised demonstrations in stimulating classroom behavior change. Several studies currently under way or recently completed suggest that the video-tape recorder may become an important tool for supervision.

Theoretical Models in Application

A persistent and growing idea colors my thinking about instructional supervision and the behavior of supervisors. This is the idea that we must borrow heavily from theory and research in the various behavioral sciences in order to develop and perfect supervision as an applied science. This is hardly a new notion, for engineering, medicine and administration have trod this same path.

Supervision is a very complex field of educational endeavor and needs desperately to borrow from a variety of fields for its theoretical models. This borrowing should be selective, obviously, and will involve adapting and amalgamating. Whatever the approach, supervisory practice needs to move toward theory-based programs which might be systematically tested, providing at least some internal consistency and inferred validity to the supervisor's efforts.

Theoretical frames of reference from which supervision might borrow are numerous. The fields of learning, psychotherapy, social change, organization, communications, and human relations, are wide open to supervisors and educational researchers in the sense that theory building has been well advanced in each. Other disciplines might well offer promise, but I shall only comment briefly on some of these.

Learning Theory

Programmed learning with its underlying notion of a stimulus-response-feedback mechanism in the teaching-learning process has been carefully conceptualized and various applications are being tested and researched. Surely, there are some aspects of the in-service education of teachers which might be approached from this frame of reference. Highly programmed in-service opportunities for experience might well be developed and tested. On the other hand, basic concepts might be borrowed from programming to employ in designing workshop or laboratory type experiences for teachers.

Recent emphasis upon the process of discovery in learning has exciting implications for supervisory practice. How can we design for discovery by teachers and others? Surely, the "workshop" as originally conceived by Kelley (18) and others was heading in this direction. Like so many ideas this was cast in bronze before being fully sculptured; hence, the workshop has generally failed to be either a thing of beauty or utility.

Education specialists in government, business and industry are borrowing heavily from learning theorists in designing training programs using reality simulation models as projections of and improvements upon the older laboratory models (30). Simulation programs have, unfortunately, come to be associated with fancy gadgetry such as the Link trainer and the paraphernalia of the astronauts. My colleagues and I have tested with promising results a number of programs using reality simulation for administrator, supervisor, and teacher in-service education (13). We have been able to limit the need for hardware and to design programs which are practical for a variety of field applications. These programs even seem to be enthusiastically received by well experienced school people who may approach anything labeled as "in-service education" with moaning, grumbling and skepticism.

Psychotherapy

Just a word about the important field of psychotherapy as it applies to designs for supervision. A most obvious fact of life is that nearly all changes in instruction involve changes in people. Many blocks to instructional innovation or even improvement seem to come from conflicting values, feelings of anxiety, and deep personal needs and drives of individuals involved. If this is so, the Rogerian model of psychotherapy and learning may well be worthy of direct application in supervisory programs.

We have examples of group therapy for supervisory purposes (1) reported in the literature, but much more extensive testing is needed. On the other hand, reports on the use of role playing for therapy, catharsis, and attitude development are to be found in a wide variety of situations, suggesting easy adaptation to supervisory practice.

Social Change

When we think of supervision practice as directed toward teacher learning, we are prone to overlook the classroom and the school as interrelated social subsystems of the larger community. Conceived as social systems, school and classroom instructional programs can be studied from the sociologist's point of view. A large body of potentially useful theory is at our disposal when we consider the models and concepts that have emerged from this discipline in recent years.

Lippitt (22) and others have offered several significant new ideas for our use regarding the role of the change agent and conditions required for his success. Rogers (26) summarizes much of what is known about the problem of diffusion of innovations, which is really a very central problem for the practicing supervisor. From studies of the acculturation process we can now borrow and adapt models for designing supervisory programs for promoting educational change as a variety of social change.

The studies of human values as individually held and group expressed systems offer guidelines for supervisory program design. Hills' (16) study is one of many which points to the middle class values that predominate in the teaching field. There appear to be real changes in teacher values occurring and variations between and among groups are substantial. These are compelling reasons for systematic study of values as they operate in the school setting. The concept of precarious values developed by Selznick (27) is a most important one for use in developing strategies for curriculum implementation. The use of the superordinate goal mechanism described by Sherif (28) has yet to be fully tested as an approach to the promotion of instructional change.

Throughout the writings of eminent sociologists, anthropologists, social psychologists, political scientists, and behavioral scientists are fascinating concepts, models and even theories with great promise for supervisory practice. Even the field of economics has recently emerged with some useful ideas. After centuries of preoccupation with money, banking, prices, and production, some exciting applications of economics to education are being suggested by theorists who are conceptualizing organizational life as the flow of resources including human resources.

Perhaps it is sufficient to say here that a *good* theory is a most useful guide to practice. We must select, adapt and test those theories we find in other disciplines, for this is a fruitful endeavor. We need not do research in a vacuum nor try to build supervision theory from scratch.

Agents for Change

The development of instructional supervision as a field of professional endeavor geared to bring about improvements in classroom practices is more than a goal, it is an imperative need. There appears to be considerable new interest in supervisors, in-service education, and curriculum development from the viewpoint of strategies for instructional change. Hopefully, we are past that period in which advocates of one curriculum project after another come forth to save our educational system. We seem to be moving, somewhat erratically, in the direction of organizing for continuous and rapid change on a broad front.

A host of critical problems is facing the schools in developing supervisory staffs and programs for this era of educational change and innovation ahead. A realistic view of these problems can facilitate both developmental and research efforts. Some of these problems can be described as follows:

1. The schools do not have recognized change agents. Supervisors have not been perceived as change agents in most school systems and have rarely functioned as such. A competent, recognized change agent group needs to be developed wherever change is to be forthcoming on a planned basis.

2. Schools are so highly domesticated as social institutions that enormous resources for the cultivation of change will be required.

3. Instructional change in the school setting is inevitably a matter of change in people. This produces difficulties not equaled in situations where change is predominately technological rather than human.

4. The bureaucratic nature of school organizations and the pivotal position of administrators in the balance of power present special problems (9). The traditional role of the school as a stabilizer in our society is changing, but the administrative structure is almost exclusively geared to maintenance activities, resisting change, and avoiding controversy or conflict.

These four problem areas are sufficient challenge for the most daring of iconoclasts. The greatest challenge is in the requirement that we learn to facilitate change with much speed, steer an educationally sound course, and simultaneously preserve the heritage of free, public, local education that is unmatched for excellence anywhere in the world.

References

1. Leo Berman. "Mental Hygiene for Educators." *Psychoanalytic Review* 40 (4): 319-32; October 1953.

2. B. J. Biddle and William Ellena, editors. *Contemporary Research on Teacher Effectiveness.* New York: Holt, Rinehart and Winston, Inc., 1964.

3. Virgil E. Blanke. "Strategies for Educational Change." *SEC Newsletter* 1: 1; September 1965.

4. Henry M. Brickell. *Organizing New York State for Educational Change.* Albany, New York: The University of the State of New York, State Department of Education, December 1961.

5. David S. Bushnell. "Needed: An Auto-Instructional Approach to Adult Education." See pages 110-15 in *The Automation of School Information Systems,* Don D. Bushnell, editor, Monograph No. 1, Washington, D.C.: Department of Audiovisual Instruction, NEA, 1964.

6. Richard O. Carlson *et al. Change Processes in the Public Schools.* Eugene,

Oregon: Center for the Advanced Study of Educational Administration, University of Oregon, 1965. Chapter 1.

7. Arthur M. Coon. "Brainstorming: A Creative Problem-Solving Technique." *Journal of Communication* 7: 3; Autumn 1957.

8. John E. Coulson. "Current Trends in Programed Instructional Research at System Development Corporation." See pages 106-10 in *The Automation of School Information Systems,* Don D. Bushnell, editor, Monograph No. 1, Washington, D.C.: Department of Audiovisual Instruction, NEA, 1964.

9. Art Gallaher, Jr. "Directed Change in Formal Organizations: The School System." In: *Change Processes in the Public Schools.* R. O. Carlson *et al.* Eugene, Oregon: Center for the Advanced Study of Educational Administration, University of Oregon, 1965. p. 37-51.

10. Ben M. Harris. "The Need for Research on Instructional Supervision." *Educational Leadership* 21 (2): 129-36; November 1963.

11. Ben M. Harris. *Supervisory Behavior in Education.* Englewood Cliffs, New Jersey: Prentice-Hall, Inc., 1963.

12. Ben M. Harris. "Supervision for Affecting Instructional Changes—Problems and Strategies." *Report of the Conference.* Department of Supervisors and Directors of Instruction. Montgomery, Alabama: State Department of Education, October 1964.

13. Ben M. Harris and Kenneth E. McIntyre. *Evaluating Pupil Performance.* Austin, Texas: Extension Teaching and Field Service Bureau, The University of Texas, 1964.

14. Ben M. Harris. "Emergence of Technical Supervision." *Educational Leadership* 22 (7): 494-96; April 1965.

14a. John K. Hemphill *et al. Administrative Performance and Personality.* New York: Bureau of Publications, Teachers College, Columbia University, 1962.

15. Richard J. Hill. *A Comparative Study of Lecture and Discussion Methods.* New York: Fund for Adult Education, 1960.

16. R. Jean Hills. "Social Class and Educational Views." *Administrator's Notebook* 10: 2; October 1961. Midwest Administration Center, The University of Chicago.

17. Floyd Hunter. *Community Power Structure: A Study of Decision Makers.* Chapel Hill: The University of North Carolina Press, 1964.

18. Earl C. Kelley. *Workshop Way of Learning.* New York: Harper and Brothers, 1951.

19. A. F. Klein. *How To Use Role Playing Effectively.* New York: Association Press, 1957.

20. Paul Lazarsfeld. *The Academic Mind.* New York: Columbia University Press, 1960.

21. J. Levine and John Butler. "Lecture vs. Group Decision in Changing Behavior." *Journal of Applied Psychology* 36 (1): 29-33; February 1952.

22. Ronald Lippitt *et al. The Dynamics of Planned Change.* New York: Harcourt, Brace & World, Inc., 1958.

23. D. M. Medley and H. E. Mitzel. *Studies of Teaching Behavior: The Refinement of Two Techniques for Observing Teachers' Classroom Behavior.* Research

Series No. 28. New York: Division of Teacher Education, Board of Education of the City of New York, 1955.

24. Matthew B. Miles, editor. *Innovation in Education*. New York: Bureau of Publications, Teacher College, Columbia University, 1964.

25. Carl R. Rogers. "Significant Learning: In Therapy and Education." *Educational Leadership* 16 (4): 232-42; January 1959.

26. E. M. Rogers. *Diffusion of Innovations*. New York: The Free Press of Glencoe, 1962.

27. Philip Selznick. *Leadership in Administration: A Sociological Interpretation*. Evanston, Illinois: Row, Peterson and Company, 1957.

28. Muzafer Sherif. "Reduction of Intergroup Conflict." *American Journal of Sociology* 53: 349-56; 1958.

29. R. M. Stogdill and C. L. Shartle. *Methods in the Study of Administrative Leadership*. Columbus, Ohio: The Ohio State University, 1955.

30. Michael Thomas, Jr. *Strategies in the Preparation of School Administrators*. A Report. National Conference of Professors of Educational Administration, August 1964.

Challenges for Supervisors

Leslee J. Bishop

EVERY age has its challenges; however, the clarity with which the challenges are perceived and the direction of the responses affect significantly the nature and the quality of the institution or culture. While subsequent events will contribute to a perspective, we can neither afford the luxury of the wait nor the consequences of precipitous response.

The current revolution of alternatives is such a confrontation. There are many needs to which we must respond; there are many new resources; there are many possible avenues of action. To affect change requires that we enter the arena of action and make choices, and be a determining as well as a responding organism. The analysis of the various issues can be found elsewhere.[1] It is the intent of this discussion to select priority items from the various problems and to indicate new resources and the consequences of their use, and to indicate tenable courses of action; not to suggest consensus but to promote dialogue.

Immediate Challenges and Responsibilities

Needed today is a new emphasis on the dynamics rather than on the stuff of curriculum. Curriculum must be restated as the act and art of the transactional, the dynamic, the personal; the confrontation, and the individualized grappling with the weight of truth; the jousting with

[1] See, for example, the following: Association for Supervision and Curriculum Development. *Role of Supervisor and Curriculum Director in a Climate of Change.* 1965 Yearbook. Robert R. Leeper, editor. Washington, D.C.: the Association, 1965.

Association for Supervision and Curriculum Development. *New Insights and the Curriculum.* 1963 Yearbook. Alexander Frazier, editor. Washington, D.C.: the Association, 1963.

wit; the creation of structure; the extraction, the utilization, and the weighing. We must plan for response, for action and interaction.

This is a private and a professional, not a machine function. We facilitate the process wherein each pupil can develop a coherent portrait of his universe. Immediately we recognize the greater challenge to teaching, to supervision and to planning. For it has not yet been proved that machines make education or that media produce curriculum.

Many who are most distressed by electronic data processing, programmed instruction or ETV are those who usually view teaching as essentially an act of transfer or transmittal. Such may have been true at the time of the hornbook. But telling is not teaching, just as hearing is not learning. Those who fear the packaged curriculum are those who believe that such packaged goodies *are* the curriculum. We must emphasize that curriculum is what emerges when resources and individual perceptions are joined; it is what happens when behavior is changing, when mind and ego meet matter and concept. Curriculum is not a jointly prepared, predigested, neatly wrapped educational package, guaranteed locally incorruptible and "teacher proof."

What is needed is a less institutionalized and a more humane environment; a more personalized curriculum and individualized learning situation; concern for relevance in terms of pupils as well as for social, intellectual and national needs.

Relevance includes a dialogue with pupils in terms of their concerns. Relevance also involves elements currently being defined by research and experimentation; in terms of experiences, modes, methods and skills of inquiry and problem solving; thinking, valuing, generalizing, computing, communicating, responding, creating. The developed skills, the memory of the experience, the competence in the method—these have durability, transferability, and, hopefully, a generative quality.[2]

A rationale is needed for education and for the youth in our society. The assorted statements of goals, purposes and tasks prevalent today do not constitute such a rationale; nor do the diverse views of those currently insisting on innovation form a coherent mandate for program or for change. Further evidence of turbulence is seen in the administrative restructuring and the organizational juggling that seek to effect change through a reordering of the institutional components, rather than through a rethinking of the basic purposes and related means.[3]

As professionals *we need a better dialogue among ourselves* and the extension of the fruits of that exchange with others also concerned. From individuals we need ideas, research, experience and recommenda-

[2] Leslee J. Bishop. "Senior High School: To What Ends?" *Educational Leadership* 23 (4) : 268; January 1966.

[3] *Ibid.*, p. 267.

tions. From the association of those people and ideas we then will develop support, emphasis, strength and leadership.

Personally, I do not think we need more professional courage. We do, however, need better ideas, insights and perspectives—we need to look at implications and consequences. For example, at no time in history has the need been so great for teachers to know process, to know media, to know pupils, to know the role of a professional. Yet we have let the universities minimize their responsibilities for the qualitative education of teachers as professionals. We have insisted that the public schools, already overburdened, assume both the intellectual and professional responsibilities of teacher education.

Supervisors, curriculum workers and public schools should insist that preservice programs equip teachers to know the structure of, and to have experienced, an area or discipline; that they understand children and the difference between the normal curve and a unique individual; that they know the new curriculum and media developments and their consequences; that they know and experience the appropriate methods of inquiry and the development of knowledge; that they have an opportunity to develop some coherent set of beliefs about education, about learners, about self; that they know that their professional education has just begun, that it is not complete.

These are not new learnings or skills that can be tacked on at the end; they must be integral to the whole experience. They are not alone the responsibility of the department of education—they are the responsibility of the whole university or teacher education institution.

In some ways the substantive climax of the ASCD 1966 Conference in San Francisco was the series of ideas discussed by William Hollister.[4] After hearing again of the dominance of the subject-centered curriculum, of structure, of establishment and "antidisestablishmentarianism," Dr. Hollister, from his background in mental health and psychiatry, reinforced vividly another *structure* with which we must be concerned—that of the human ego, encompassing the mind and heart and muscles, and together comprising the entity of each one. We must continue to emphasize the fact that each individual has his worthy intellectual and emotional—being or ego—structure as defined; that to cope with the pressures on youth, the "cognitive overload," the structure of thinking, believing, behaving and becoming should also be developed as

---

[4] William G. Hollister, M.D. "Preparing the Minds of the Future: Enhancing Ego Processes Through Curriculum Development." *Curriculum Change: Direction and Process.* Robert R. Leeper, editor. Washington, D.C.: Association for Supervision and Curriculum Development, 1966. p. 27-42.

part of our teaching and learning activities and this should be done within the context of our present courses of English, mathematics, science and music and the rest. This is one element of a frontier area in which ASCD must continue to be aggressive.

We realize again the significant opportunity the Association for Supervision and Curriculum Development has in promoting the knowledge of and the commitment to the components and the structure of self, of each, of each ego as a universe deserving respect and study.

No more let structure denote only organized and funded knowledge, however worthy. Let discussions of structure also include the becomingness of each unique self, of each precious ego and its development, nurture, dimension, being and becoming.

We must study the individual as an entity as we study a discipline or a social problem. We must deal with the question: How do we marshal the resources of our environment for the development of this person? New knowledge and technology make it feasible to organize education *around the individual* if we choose to do so, rather than just around subjects, grade levels or conventional institutional remnants. If we were to spend as much time studying children and youth as we do French or physics, we would indeed have a revolution in education. On this problem we must provide leadership.

What service, what leadership can ASCD give to the immediate and consequential dimension of leadership in international education? Our world is only 60 minutes in circumference and a pair of human eyes can look upon a hemisphere. More and more Americans are abroad in various educational and military capacities. New ideas or good ideas can be communicated instantly in visual and auditory form. We do not have to wait for print; we do not have to wait for translation. The only delay is caused by our own lack of ingenuity, imagination and commitment.

Just as the helicopter has revolutionized warfare by making it possible to put men any place on the globe in a short time without hacking through jungles, climbing mountains, or traversing long stretches of desert, or water, so TV and communication satellites now make it possible to put information, help or inspiration at any point in the world. We either participate in this development or watch others make it happen. I recommend that we participate, not by proliferating our energies through initiating a new series of commissions and a new series of tasks, but by incorporating the international dimension more intimately and more clearly into what we do, by contributing to the flow of ideas without regard to race, color, creed, sex or political boundaries.

What is our concept of the teacher: What is the teacher? A technician or a perceptive professional? What does a teacher do? Confront and interact—or drill and manipulate?

Much has been written of the new role of the teacher as the coordinator of an expanding series of services and facilities used to enhance the learning of each pupil; as a specialist team member who participates in large and small group sessions and teams with others to share competencies and interests; as the producer and dispenser of multidimensional media that spread knowledge and analyze feedback; as the leader in a process of inquiry whereby pupils are encouraged to discover generalizations, to relate knowledge to broader concepts and to understand the various disciplines as they become producers of knowledge.[5]

Our concept of the teacher, or teaching, of learners and learning will determine how we perform as supervisors.

There are many new roles for coordinators and supervisors: there are the *coordinators* of federal programs; the liaison person between the university or school and the regional laboratory or center; there are those who work with local, state or national agencies and institutions; those with lay and parent or neighborhood and civic groups; the Peace Corps, Neighborhood Youth Corps, the Job Corps; the area vocational or technical school, the community college; the local business and industrial powers. These are extensions of old, and dimensions of new tasks —and the old formulas, roles and functions are not enough to do the job today.

Supervision is also changing because of new media, new instructional devices, new and far-reaching studies of the teaching-learning act,[6] and new emphasis on the importance of individual perceptions. Research capabilities, new instruments and media tend to reinforce the need for more insight, more personal facilitation, and more in-service work of a helping nature. Changes coming from new and powerful forces require knowledge of change processes, and competence on the part of the supervisor as the agent of change. These and many other realities suggest that the supervisors working with teachers in these activities today also have new roles, new tools, new responsibilities. We must grasp this significant responsibility before we lose it—the task is to research it, delineate it, nurture it, professionalize it.

[5] Helen Heffernan and Leslee J. Bishop. "The Supervisor and Curriculum Director at Work." *Role of Supervisor and Curriculum Director in a Climate of Change.* Robert R. Leeper, editor. Washington, D.C.: Association for Supervision and Curriculum Development, 1965. p. 135.

[6] Louise M. Berman and Mary Lou Usery. *Personalized Supervision: Sources & Insights.* Washington, D.C.: Association for Supervision and Curriculum Development, 1966.

What do we do? It is our special business and responsibility—

To know what curriculum is and what is not. To decide what we want and to say so

To know how learners learn, and how they are best taught, and helped to learn

To know what school is, what it is for, and for whom it exists

To know how decisions are made, and by whom and for what

To establish liaison among ourselves, and with government, industry and community

To face change, and the new role these responsibilities involve.

What are supervisors, curriculum workers for? As a starter . . . we should stand for—

A workable and behaviorally-oriented philosophy of education

A teachable group, a learning group

Accessible media, materials and resources

Administrative and supervisory support

Community cooperation and understanding

Meaningful student data for diagnosis and remediation

A concern for the individual—be he learner or teacher

Time for preparation, implementation and follow-through

An open, developed and accessible decision-making process.

All aspects of education, all ways of operating are being revised because of the knowledge explosion, the technological explosion, the revolution in values, and the explosion of expectancies. The collection and dissemination of data are an imminent spin-off from the shotgun marriage of the knowledge explosion and technology. This development is a creature already spawned and about to be born full-blown; it will not enjoy the luxury of infancy or the experimentation of adolescence. For some it will come as a thief in the night. For those who anticipate, it can be a welcome resource for decision making, for individualizing the school program, for depth analysis of the many over-generalized and under-researched areas in education.

Long Range Challenges in Supervision

Awe and anticipation are usually the first reactions to the fantastic output. The input maw will, of necessity, draw time and talent from essential tasks postponed by the omnivorous appetite of the new beast. Eventually it will be tamed, some balance will be achieved, and selective and qualitative considerations will become possible.

We are today developing the capacity to manipulate fantastic amounts of data with innumerable variables. This new potentiality has direct implications for all persons involved in the educational enterprise. Supervisors, curriculum directors, department chairmen and administrators traditionally have been responsible for the collection, collating, analysis, communication and implementation of many levels of data such as—

Textbooks; their selection, use, replacement

Curriculum materials; procurement and inventory

Materials; production, selection and distribution

Communication; regarding studies, activities, research, promising practices

Skills sessions; for A-V use or production, teacher competencies and extent of classroom use

In-service activities; involving information sharing, coordination

Collection and analysis of data; regarding teacher training, competencies regarding subject or skill, selection for responsibility where qualifications or experience are the most significant factors.

These responsibilities and roles and many similar ones will soon be nonexistent, or handled by para-professionals, technicians, computers or programs.

Unfortunately, in many school systems, supervisors and many curriculum workers may have become a part of a place-holding operation. In the past a complex need has resulted in the naming of someone to somehow reconcile the many responsibilities and unmet overarching tasks; and the caretaker of these varied needs was often called a supervisor or coordinator. As the place-holder for a gap that existed, it was hoped that the person would provide the spark necessary to leap the gap. However necessary the tasks, a mystique pervaded this supervisory responsibility which often was undefined to or by the place-holder or other persons in the system. Programming and systems analysis today may dissolve such a house built upon sand.

Once the roles of all the professionals in a system are exploded into form and exposed as to function, the nature of the decision making, the uses of time, the relationship to necessary timing and responsibilities, these elements will be public knowledge—and subject to exacting review and investigation. Also, when the functions of administrative, curriculum development, and supervisory persons are delineated, we may find that many roles are logical in a design but not in an actual situation. Such study and delineation will require changes and decisions regarding the various roles or their placement in the administrative structure.

This system procedure or automated new orientation, reinforced by the research thrust which presently dominates the scene, may, in large measure, determine the relationship of objectives and values. Inspired by both the capacity of cybernetics and the methodology of the Pentagon is the growing pattern of establishing: (a) carefully determined targets; then (b) highly refined objectives; and (c) possible or potential courses of action to be pursued. In this procedure an "effectiveness cost" factor can be determined for each goal or each alternative. Outcomes tend to be technically structured and data-oriented. Values that are not included in the operational mode or the objective will be lost or obscured; a value interpretation at the end of the process is too late. Supervisors and curriculum workers must develop new ways of thinking or proceduring whereby we build values into the beginning, the hypothesis, the objectives and the procedures. This intense and highly focused procedure is obviously quite in contrast to many of our present generalized functions and responsibilities.

Now let us look at values. Unfortunately, the impact of these procedures will become generally known at about the same time that the developing value-crisis has reached its climax; the automobile, vocational change and obsolescence, urbanization, science in outer space, leisure, "the pill," drug and genetic manipulation will have made value agreements and orientation significantly less stable and more tenuous.

Professionals concerned with these developments must make a concerted effort if human and human relations aspects are also built into the system. Values and human relations are not likely to be the concerns of the researcher, the technician or the statistician. It is the responsibility of the supervisor to see that humane concerns are implicit in the tables, dial readings and implications of each research objective and each spun-out consequence.

Studies of the teaching act, the learning act, environmental effects and components of achievement make a concern for *precision* inevitable and expected. Rather than react negatively, we should welcome the potential for feedback and review; we should welcome the opportunity to develop creative, innovative and personalized strategies—for teaching, for learning, for supervision. Computer analysis will anticipate many actions; simulated procedures can eliminate many skill and perceptual problems in training.

So, we can expect a new data-oriented and computer-programmed environment into which we will feed extrapolated procedures and practices developed by thoughtful, knowledgeable and well-financed curriculum producers—highly sophisticated, with many alternatives and possibilities, many related and supplementary possibilities. The *supervisor* will research and select, modify, add, adapt, evaluate and revise. This will require a highly trained and flexible mind, an empathetic and perceptive spirit.

The teacher, as a specialist in individual growth and a coordinator of educational media and resources, will require different kinds of help and supervision than are now available. The teaching act will be diversified, but characterized by individualized analysis, confrontation, development and remediation. Aided by media and resources including a vast array of technical resources, the teacher will not program each child. Rather each child will have programmed resources, in part selected by the child, by the teacher and the supervisor. They will be educationally telemetered—a cybernated diagnosis, designed to move each learner forward with appropriate speed, with consideration for success and satisfaction.

The drillmaster, if one is needed, will be the para-professional, the technician, the simulator or the program. The teacher will be the facilitator, the guide, the analyzer. If we anticipate our responsibility, these depersonalized resources and automated capacities will represent facilities, *not* objectives, goals or significant requirements. Teaching, learning and supervision must properly transcend these depersonalized means, and instead be highly personal, highly individualized and value-oriented. This hoped for outcome requires a change in the teaching role of many, and a dramatic reorientation for many supervisors and administrators.

Finally let us look at existence itself or at the survival of our role. We know that many planning functions will be modified, and that essential decisions will be made on higher and higher levels by those who have access to any and all of the data flow. We know that the reporting, maintenance, data-correlating and information-coordination will be done by technicians or those in lesser roles. As stated, accessibility to the data will be the key element; the collection and dissemination of data will be based on a high-level decision, but will not constitute a high-level responsibility of a continuing nature as it now does.

One strategic function to watch carefully will be the determination and control of *non*-automated data and decision making. This small, but personal element may be one creative and humane element and one hopefully to be determined by the supervisor. Either the pressure to automate, or the determination to traditionalize this component, must constantly be analyzed.

In addition to depersonalization and fragmentation, the development of wide personal role gaps also looms as a potential danger. We see evidences now of a split between the producer and user of curriculum resources, between the researcher and the practitioner, between the government and the local system, between the teacher and the supervisor or administrator, between the student and the school, between the generations.

The impasse currently developing because of the new aggressiveness of the teacher in welfare and professional matters must also be our concern. Pressures now exist to split the teacher from the supervisor, the curriculum worker, the administrator. However important we think the team approach to curriculum decision and policy formulation may be, the teacher has felt significantly excluded from these considerations and is striking back. The reaction is not all negative—primarily it is a determination to be a full-fledged professional. But a significant portion of a struggle for conditions of employment and teaching responsibility contributes directly to a split in function, to a dual force rather than a unified product. Unless something intervenes, unless a voice or a force not now evident appears, it may not be long before teachers and supervisors are in different associations. I believe the situation will get worse before it gets better. The likelihood exists that the breach currently being developed will widen and not be closed in our professional lifetime.

Thus at the same time that the potential depersonalizing forces of technology are increasing, so are conflicts in the strategies for change as perceived by teachers, local associations, government, business interests and societies of scholars. The time to heal the developing breach is the immediate present, before further restrictive procedures are determined and policies built into legislation and school board action.

The intent, therefore, of these statements is not to foment further intramural conflicts among ourselves, but to observe, and if possible to analyze the lines of force rapidly freezing into a new untenable situation.

The new voices from the streets, from industrial complexes, from government, from scholars, from learners and from the teachers will not be muted. What shall we do? I suggest that we should:

1. Seek out those curriculum developments and centers that we believe are sound and worthy and cooperate with them—including commercial, research and university consortia

2. Become more aggressive as spokesmen for good teaching-learning situations and procedures, for individualizing instruction by whatever means—including administrative, mechanical or para-professional

3. Support teacher education institutions, many of which are at their lowest ebb in personnel, status and voice in determining program or emphasis. Insist that college classroom experience is not enough, that teaching is more than knowing

4. Recognize that education is big business, is public; that business is in it; that education is a social force as well as an institutional responsibility; that forces outside the school may be pervasive ones for the foreseeable future

5. Organize to operate in a political arena, study legislative proposals, be willing to review what the states, U. S. Office of Education, or the Office of Economic Opportunity is proposing; and to act

6. Open our eyes and ears to the voices from the streets, the ghettos, the disadvantaged, the less-than-bright; know the currents of change and their likely impact upon the local or national scene

7. Be flexible with our ideas, our curriculum, our policies and procedures; build in procedures for change; include teachers and lay citizens in our planning of strategies and processes

8. Revise our understanding of the role of the school and the professional, knowing that the lay citizen has ideas, insights, experiences; that he has his children in his schools; maintain an open school, an open classroom and a joint enterprise

9. Recognize our unique responsibility for ideas; for leadership; that we must stand for the best we know, not for the most easily managed or cheaply financed

10. Help sustain humane values in an increasingly numerical, automated environment; promote a learning society in which individuals count; see education as a process and a possibility; promote valuing as well as achievement.

These are difficult tasks. Nevertheless, those tasks to which we address ourselves and which we affect significantly will determine our role in the school and our role in society. We have this opportunity to shape our professional and personal destiny. How we use this opportunity will largely determine who we are and what we will become.

Organizational Factors in Supervision[1]

James G. March

LET us start by looking at the problem of organizational design as it has been viewed classically. Then I will report on some research on organizational decision making as one way of approaching the problem of organizational design. Finally I will try to draw some implications for supervision that come out of this research. I hope the reader will bear with me as I refer to business organizations and other kinds of institutions because I think there is a point to be made and eventually I expect to get there. Let me start out by talking about organizational design.

Organizational design, classically, starts with something called an organization chart, which is, allegedly, a description of an organization. The organization chart consists of two things: a set of rectangles and a set of directed arrows. The rectangles, traditionally, have referred either to individuals or to roles and the arrows, traditionally, have been interpreted as meaning "reports to," "hires," and "fires," or "has authority over," etc.

With these organization charts or associated with them, at least, are a set of what one could call "organizational homilies"; proverbs, as one of my colleagues has called them, such as, "authority should be commensurate with responsibility"; "one man should have only one

---

[1] This presentation was made at the ASCD Curriculum Research Institute from notes and was later transcribed from a tape recording. In authorizing the publication here, I apologize for two conspicuous faults. First, the English is execrable. Rather than attempt the major rewriting job that would be required to make it reasonable, I preface it with this apology. Second, it is unfootnoted. The talk draws heavily upon research done jointly with a number of colleagues, most conspicuously Richard M. Cyert and Herbert A. Simon. They should be absolved, however, from the implications drawn for supervision in the last few paragraphs.—JGM.

boss"; and "the span of control should be neither too large nor too small" (which means that there should be some number less than infinity, but greater than one, arrows coming out of each box). If you read the management literature, I think you are compelled sometimes to have the feeling that you are reading Polonius's advice to Laertes and that this writing has all of the wisdom and all of the irrelevance of that advice. It is easy to poke fun at organization charts. It is easy to poke fun at the proverbs of organization. For one thing, the proverbs tend to come in pairs. There is a proverb that says you should keep the number of levels in the organization small and another that you should have a fixed number of positions. You just cannot do both simultaneously. It is also easy to poke fun at the poverty of description involved in organization charts and various people have proposed a variety of alternatives.

It has been proposed, mostly by economists, that the proper way to describe an organization is in terms of its task structure: that there are various jobs, that these jobs can be specified and then can be grouped together and that an organization consists of the grouping of these jobs and the relations among them. This is a procedure that has been used in the theory of the firms, producing things like the production function. It produces some relatively interesting theoretical notions but as far as I know has never been of very much use to a manager.

Organization as Decision-Making Structure

We can view the organization as a communication structure. Instead of describing the organization as a set of boxes and arrows, we described it as either another different set of boxes and arrows or perhaps more elegantly, as an array of "who-talks-to-whom." If we put that array in the proper form we can then operate on it algebraically, and we can make statements such as, "who is removed from whom by how many links," and we may get some insights in the ways of modifying that organization that way. We can describe an organization as a sociometric network—"who likes whom" or "who would like to work with whom" or who and whatever kind of question you want to ask a group of organization members. This has actually been done and some forms of organization design have been built upon it, particularly in reform institutions. But I want to focus on a fourth alternative way of describing the organization. And that is the organization as a decision-making structure.

Why would one want to describe an organization as a decision-making structure? If you are talking about business organizations, that is fairly self-evident and the answer is fairly self-evident. Business organizations deal in decisions or they appear to. They make decisions on price, on output, on advertising strategy, on investment, on allocation of resources, and this seems to be the heart of what goes on in the business organization. So if you want to predict the heart of what goes on in the business organization, you may very well be interested in this decision-making structure. But this function is less compelling, perhaps, for an organization such as an educational institution, although I am prepared to argue here, too, that it is compelling. A second reason, which I think is even more compelling and more relevant to our concerns, is that presumably if you are interested in change or innovation in an organization, then change and innovation generally can be viewed as kinds of decisions made by the organization. One of the things that may come out of a study of the decision-making structure is some knowledge about what characterizes an innovative organization.

There are some classic approaches to theories of decision making in organization. Perhaps the most classic, the one with which I think we instinctively deal, or perhaps automatically deal, is what I would call the economic managerial model of organizational decision making. This is a fairly straightforward model that comes out of economics or is used widely in economics. It is assumed there is some person who in economics would be called entrepreneur. This kind of control group or person who has some objectives would then purchase some employees for wages or other rewards of one sort or another. In return for these inducements the employee agrees to share the objectives of the entrepreneur. The problem then becomes one of the entrepreneur making rational decisions in the face of uncertainty and implementing these decisions through the organization. I think this is the classic model in economics. It is also the classic model in managerial theory. As I will point out a little later, this is by and large the model on which most notions of supervision are built.

This model assumes a basic asymmetry between the entrepreneur or the manager, or whoever you want to talk about and the employee. It assumes that via some pattern of inducements, the employee or the participant, whatever he may be, comes to accept the authority or the objectives of the entrepreneur or the control group. This reduces the problems of organizational decision making immediately into the problems of individual decision making. This also permits the economist and others interested in organizational decision making from this point of view to talk about firms as though they were individuals; to talk about rational organizational decision making in the same terms using exactly the same concepts as those views in theories of rational individual choice.

The second classic approach to decision making (organizational decision making) is a little different; it comes more out of a political, sociological position and is basically a power model. It assumes that within the organization there are various groups and individuals, that these groups and individuals, for some reasons that are extraneous to the organization, have something called power which for all the world is a number hung around their neck and says, "my power is sixty-seven," that when they come together they compare powers or weight their individual opinions by the power, and that the outcome (the decision) is the weighted average of those initial positions where the weights are the powers. Once the decision is made, via this route, then the problem becomes one of implementing through rewards, inducements, direction, and so on. This model, which has led to a rather elaborate literature on measurement of power, can be found in much of the traditional literature that comes out of political science and a fairly substantial part of the traditional literature that comes out of sociology. This, then, is the background to our own efforts to develop a reasonable set of models of decision making in organizations.

Let us now refer to our research, since it might conceivably be relevant. This research has proceeded on four different fronts. First we have engaged in a number of extended field studies of organizations making decisions—business organizations making decisions on the allocation of resources, governmental organizations making decisions on price and output, and business organizations making decisions on investment. There have been a variety of sneaky and open ways in which we have observed organizations. These ways have ranged from field studies lasting more than a year in a single organization to fairly brief looks at some organization records and relatively brief interviews with some organizations.

The second thing we have done is to take data on organization decisions and analyze these essentially in a statistical way to establish, to develop a model or alternate model, and to test these models against the data that are readily or fairly readily, publicly available.

The third thing we have done in some areas where it has seemed to us critical for the theory to know something about the dynamics of organizations, is to develop some laboratory experiments studying small parts of organizations. For example, the processing of information under partial conflict of interest. And the fourth thing that we have done is to try to take the data from all of these studies, develop models, mathematical and computer models, of what goes on in the organization and attempt to use those models to predict the decisions within an organization. I wanted to mention five such models that we have developed, and by this we mean a group—a loose group of economists, psychologists, sociologists, and unidentified professional objects, who have operated on organizations over the past five years, roughly. The first is a model of output determination in the can industry.

The can industry is basically a duopoly, at the moment occupied almost entirely by the American Can Company and the Continental Can Company, who divided 85-90 percent of the market, of the American market at least. About the turn of the century and up to about 1910, this market was a monopoly of American Can. What we attempted to do was to take data on the share of market and the profit ratios of American Can Company and Continental Can Company, which started about 1910, over the 1910-1960 period, roughly, and attempted to develop a model of how decisions got made in those organizations. That in conjunction with a reasonable model of the market would produce a prediction of the share of market and profit ratios of these two firms.

To do this we essentially speculated, on the basis of our other observations of organizations, on what kind of processes would go on in a new business firm as opposed to what kind of processes would go on in an old established firm. We speculated about the kinds of information that would be used to make these decisions and how that information would be related. We speculated, in short, about the decision process within these two firms without ever going inside the firms themselves. This model, which has now been published, predicts reasonably well both the share of the market and the profit shares of American Can and Continental Can Company over that 40 or 50 year period. It makes some errors and, regrettably, the statistical techniques for testing the goodness or fit of computer models, which this turned out to be, with actual data are not well enough established to say with confidence whether those errors are major ones or minor ones. Most of our colleagues and certainly we ourselves seem to believe that the fit is good, considering the crudity of the model.

The second model to be mentioned here was quite different in motivation though remarkably similar in structure. We spent over a year studying intensively what went on in a department store as it set prices and ordered goods. This was obviously a practical problem to help our wives who want to know the optimal time to buy ladies' ready-to-wear and I believe we determined what the optimal time was. What we did was to plant a stool pigeon, openly, in the store. He was not a CIA agent; he was more like a Department of State representative. He was there.

He observed what went on. Among other duties, he observed on a day-to-day basis what a group of buyers did.

Out of this we developed, again a computer model of what went on in this department store, how it sets prices, how it orders and then compared this with the actual pricing and purchase behavior of this department store, with results that I think are on the whole rather spectacular in the sense that we were able to predict the prices that would be set, correct to the penny anywhere from 91-99 percent of the time depending upon the kind of tastes we are talking about, whether we are referring to pricing for sales or pricing for regular day-to-day purchasing.

A third kind of model is a model of investment in the trust department of a bank. Here we went, openly and over a period of time, into the trust department. We met, as we met in all of these organizations, very sophisticated decision makers—any time you get close to the stock market you get a grand mystique of navel contemplation and other important tools of the stock purchaser. We attempted to develop a model that would simulate the behavior of this particular trust department.

Geoffrey Clarkson was able to build a model that very closely simulated the portfolio purchase behavior of the trust department. In fact, in one case, his model made an error which the trust department decided was their error not his, that they had just done their arithmetic poorly. By and large he predicted complete portfolios correctly, exactly correctly, or in some cases his model would buy a hundred shares of Duquesne Light rather than a hundred shares of Southeastern Power. The trust officer was sufficiently impressed by this to be concerned. Several banks have been sufficiently impressed to try to use this to implement their own decisions. Again it used a model that was formerly very similar —and I will come to some of the characteristics of those models later— to the department store model or the can industry model.

Fourth, we attempted to develop, and here we were less successful, a model for allocation to research and development which actually is a simpler task and which I think we can do fairly easily; but allocation is to be made to particular objects within a research and development budget. Although we were able to predict fairly well for one particular organization in which we spent a good deal of time, we were unable to develop a reasonable model of prediction for two other organizations in which we spent comparable amounts of time. One of the key problems that we face in developing models of research and development is the ambiguity of the labels that are put on budget items. Most of these organizations put labels on projects like "research in polymer chemistry," or "basic research in microbiology." As we got into these projects, however, it became fairly clear that what was basic research on microbiology one year got labeled "applied research in polymers," the next year, and until we could crack that labeling problem, which we never did, we would have difficulty developing a complete model in that area.

Fifth, we have developed our study without direct observation of any specific firm, but we have tried to pull together, through observations from these various models and from other studies of firms, what we call a general model of price and output determination in a modern American firm. We then have attempted to use this model to predict some gross aggregate variation and behavior within American firms. We also have tried to state some assumptions, make some predictions about what kinds of firms will, for example, innovate with respect to technology under what circumstances; what kinds of firms are likely to get into antitrust difficulties under what circumstances; and what kinds of governmental stimulation of the economy will have what kinds of effects upon various firms. In these essentially policy kinds of propositions, we have attempted at least to test our models. In some cases we have been right and in other cases we have been wrong, which is encouraging because it is not very good to have a model that always works, in fact this is never good.

Characteristics of the Models

What are the general characteristics of these models of the phenomena that we think we have discovered? The classic economic model of rational decision making in an organization says that an organization at any point in time has a criterion function, or a goal, a well-defined, well-specified, objective. The organization knows all alternatives, it evaluates those alternatives by evaluating all possible consequences or at least the probability distribution on all possible consequences, and selects that alternative that maximizes the criterion function of the objective or, if it is a probability distribution, it maximizes the expected value of that function.

What did we find? First, with respect to criteria, or goals or objectives, the most conspicuous thing is that all of the organizations with which we dealt had multiple, changing, conflicting goals. They were inconsistent over time; what the organization did today was inconsistent with what it did yesterday. There were inconsistencies within the organization; what was happening in the sales department was inconsistent with what was happening in the production department. This was as conspicuous as anything could be in looking at business organizations and governmental organizations. They did not have a single well-defined goal. Yet they survived reasonably well.

How did these organizations survive? One way in which they survived was that they had the goals specified in terms of aspiration levels rather than in terms of maximizing a function. Instead of saying we want the maximum profit, they had an aspiration level. With respect to profit we want a profit or return on investment or share of the market or whatever of such and such a level. How does this help? It helps most conspicuously because they may understate their possibility and they can absorb some of the inconsistency and objectives by the slack that is produced by understating their objectives relative to what they could achieve. So they could tolerate having part of the organization working for sales, another part working for profit, and another part working for smooth employment patterns because they never have to face the really critical issue of how much of which do you want to give up for the other, because as long as the world was relatively benign according to their aspiration levels, they did not have to face this problem.

A second way in which the organizations survived in the face of multiple, conflicting, changing objectives, was by what could only be described as sequential attention to goals. The organization looked as though it attended one moment to one goal, the next moment to another goal, and once it had taken care of goal one, those people who were concerned about that retreated into the woods and then we worried about goal two, and those people who were concerned about that made decisions that then were inconsistent with goal one which would eventually reactivate the people who were interested before. By that time, the people interested in goal two would be out of it. Thus we have, I suppose, the department store or the trust officers in the bank behaving much the way I would assume a reasonable high school principal does—that he makes a set of decisions for parents and then hopes they will hide before he has to deal with teachers so that he can then make a set of decisions for teachers that will satisfy them, so he can go off and deal with supervisors and if he can just keep one step ahead of the consequences of his decisions, over time, everyone is satisfied although he is making strictly inconsistent decisions. And that is the way these organizations behave.

With respect to their goals, these were changing, multiple, inconsistent. We also discovered in our study that we went in with very naïve notions of what a goal is. We assumed, along with most economists, that there are things that are objectives of a reasonable business firm, like profit, and that this is what makes the system go. We discovered in a business firm where I suppose we would feel least likely to discover it, even more obviously in a governmental organization, that all of these goals and all the goals that are stated in the annual report are remarkably non-operational. They might just as well say that our objective is to do good, and, of course, some of them do say this. Even the profit goal, which sounds very concrete, very specific, very hard headed, turns out to be quite elusive because what you want within the organization is the marginal contribution of profit made by the production department and nobody knows how to calculate that. So what do you use? Well for all the world the organization seems to be wandering around searching for cues as to what it might use as goals and it discovers some fairly simple things, such as these: If the antitrust division of the Department of Justice calls in the morning, drop everything, organize your attorneys, call your vice-presidents together, get to work!

The only way I can interpret this is that a major goal of the organization, an organization in which I observed, is to minimize telephone calls from the antitrust division of the Department of Justice. And, in fact, that is how they behave. Actually, for all practical purposes, that is their goal. We observed in one organization, engaged in a cost-cutting campaign, contests for successful cost-cutting departments. The goal of each department, because they were getting rewarded, was to cut costs. Well, late one afternoon I was talking in a somewhat dimly lit bar with the company champion in cost-cutting. This was the manager of the department which had just won the prize for cutting costs. He finally explained to me how they did it. They had cracked the code. They had figured out how people were calculating, what was getting cut, how costs were getting cut, and they had very carefully reallocated things, so that those things that were counted they were cutting and those things that were not counted they were adding to. This department had, in fact, pursued its real goal which was to minimize costs as calculated by a particular objective.

We got into something called the automobile industry. Many of the automobile industries now have "profit centers." There is a Buick profit center, I think, and a Chevrolet profit center, and the manager of the Buick Division is evaluated in terms of what his profits are. What determines what his profits are? At least in the organization we were looking at, which did not happen to be General Motors, what seemed to determine the profits of the divisional managers was what "transfer prices" they could negotiate with the other divisions. Most of what was scored as profit came from transfers that were strictly accounting transfers: How much does this division pay to that other division for things we get from them? So the managers spent most of their time bargaining about how transfer prices were determined and how overhead was allocated; because if they could ever win these two battles, nothing they did otherwise made any difference. From the point of view of the overall organization, if there is such a thing, this is slightly peculiar because it says that the manager of the Buick Division spent most of his time trying to increase his profit at the expense of the Chevrolet Division and that is the easiest way he has for increasing his profit. He simply looks at the accounting system and he says, "That's where I've got some possibilities," and so he goes.

Throughout all of these organizations we were able to see things that triggered action in one area or another. All organizations have "safety goals." Very few business organizations spend any time at all worrying about safety, although the annual report will explain how safe they are. Yet there are certain times when these organizations spend an enormous amount of time worrying about safety. One such time is when they kill somebody. So we happened to observe an organization right after they managed to manipulate a crane so that it had crushed someone to death. Suddenly the whole organization was worried about safety. They said, "Safety is our most important product. We've got to be safe," and somebody else held other meetings and the safety statistics were improved. Two months later there were other problems so they were onto other things and the decisions they had made by that time were changed for other reasons and they were backed, but we could see very clearly that safety was a goal of this organization as long as someone was killed regularly.

This is the kind of flavor that one could get about goals in this kind of organization. In general, the kind of picture one got was of a business organization as a kind of loose coalition between a variety of groups or among a variety of groups, each group having some objectives which it would like to achieve more or less at the expense of the other groups and to achieve these whenever it could. The total organizational objectives were somehow this whole messy package of individual constraints imposed upon the system. So much for the nice consistent operational criterion.

The second assumption of the classical economic model is that all alternatives are known and the information about all alternatives is known. Well, it is very clear that this is not true either. The most conspicuous thing here is that all of the organizations we looked at considered only a very small number of alternatives before making a decision. They did not generate many alternatives. They generated the existing one usually and perhaps an alternative one. They found that the alternatives did not come to them magically from on high; that they had to search for them, and that they searched for them in a rather consistent way. They searched when faced with a problem as we defined it by failure on some goal. They searched in the neighborhood of the present solution, and they searched with a substantial bias—the bias predictable from knowledge about who is searching. Then to give you some flavor of the search process, let me describe our picture of what happened again when someone was killed in a particular major American firm.

A trigger went off! An alarm went off! There was a fire! Not a literal fire, but a fire in safety, somebody got killed. There must be something wrong with our safety procedure. We'll have a conference. We hold a conference, everybody thrashes around; they try to find out what happened in this particular case. What apparently happened as nearly as we can tell in this particular case was a kind of more or less chance event, a workman was where he should not have been and a crane operator probably should have looked, but he had been working that way all the time and the crane went where he told it to go and somebody was there. There were some causal factors, but they were not very conspicuously causal factors that one could improve on. So we had a conference and things broke off with the words, "We have to do something about safety!"

Meanwhile back in the manufacturing department, there was an engineer, in fact there was a whole group of engineers who had a pet project they had been trying to sell to management for many months, which had to do with automatic cranes. They get this bulletin that says something about safety and, since we had killed somebody with one of the older cranes, they put one and one together and got six, and said, "Ah, maybe these cranes, these nice new automatic cranes should be sold to management as a safety device!" So they came up with an alternative—the way to solve this problem is to put in the new automatic crane. Well, it did solve the problem. Not in the sense that it made any difference to the accident. This accident would have occurred with or without the automatic crane. But it solved what was the real problem, which was some kind of action that would relieve people's feeling that they were not doing anything about safety. It also solved the engineers' problem, which was how to sell automatic cranes when they are obviously un-economical. So a major managerial decision was made, "We are going to implement cranes. That solves the problem." Anytime anybody says, "What are you doing about safety after that accident?" "We are putting in new cranes," and they start implementing.

Six months later they stopped implementing cranes. Why? Because there was now a new emergency, which was: we have to save money. We are running out of money, where can we save money, and suddenly we say, "Well what are we buying all those new cranes for? They look expensive, so we can cut back on cranes." The results were that the engineers got three or four new cranes, we solved the safety problem and we solved the money saving problem.

In classical economic theory, a business organization deals with uncertainty by calculating the probability distribution of various events and then computing the expected value return for various alternatives. We believe, however, that in actual practice most of the organizations we looked at ran away from uncertainty with great vigor. They avoided it rather than dealt with it. They avoided it by creating elaborate standard procedures, rather than being uncertain about what that other department might do and calculating some sort of probability as to what that department might do. They said, in effect: "Let's create some procedures so we'll know with some certainty what the department will do. Of course along the way, what we'll do is to constrain the department considerably so that it cannot do something it might want to do or maybe it should do. Let's delay as long as possible a decision that depends upon uncertain future events so that in ordering goods, rather than trying to guess what the market will be, we'll try to delay as long as possible and then make a decision even though it costs us a little more in terms of the prices we will have to pay. If we are dealing with other firms, let's collude."

Collusion comes in lots of different categories. One form of collusion in a business organization is to meet at the Duquesne Club or Petroleum Club and sit down and say, "Well you take this much of the market and I'll take that much of the market and so on." That kind of collusion is frowned upon in some quarters and so there are a variety of other collusions that in fact are not even viewed as collusions.

One form of collusion is to develop standard operating procedures in accounting. Now we developed standard operating procedures in accounting and got the various accountants to accept them. This simplifies our life a good deal because we know what our costs are then. We know a lot more about what our costs are than we would know otherwise. So we observed, for example, one day a department store buyer in one department store calling up the department store buyer in other department stores and saying, "Jack, you made a mistake. You have too low a price on those goods." And Jack said, "My gosh, you're right, I do!" and immediately raised it. There are several alternative explanations of what that particular message was being sent for. Yet I think what was actually being said was close to what was intended to be said. I do not think this was kind of an elaborate way of saying, "You scratch my back and I'll scratch yours" or "Come on, don't be cutting prices on me this week, I'm in trouble." It was just that he knew that if the other man in the other organization was following the standard operating procedures, he had arrived at a wrong conclusion and he felt he ought to help him out.

We found in department stores that one department store was paying a fairly substantial amount of money for an economic forecast of demand which it then, by an elaborate process of mumbo-jumbo, did absolutely nothing with. All right, so we have goals, we have information, we have decisions. In the classic economic theories, decision is straightforward, you take the information, you compare it with the goals, and you maximize the criteria. What we, in fact, observed were organizations that were first of all dominated by historical rule. They had a whole set of elaborate rules that they had learned over time. No member of the present organization knew where those rules came from but he knew that that was how things were done and once you had captured all of those rules you had really captured most of the decisions. In fact, it was hard even to talk about decision. We discovered it was increasingly difficult to say when a decision was made. Instead of a decision in the classic economic sense, what you seemed to get was a process of gradual commitment to a course of action. We studied a decision by a major firm, early in the computer days, to buy a computer. This firm followed a process each step of which seemed to proceed rather naturally from the preceding step and no step of which was decisive but in the whole flow of events led the firm ultimately to purchase the computer.

We also seem to find in decisions, in actual decisions, that organizations substantially avoid opportunity costs, that is the cost of things that we might have done but did not do. They exaggerate in an economic sense the importance of out-of-pocket costs as easily observable costs. This means that they tend to come down hard on inconsistency, on waste—that is, waste meaning things you bought and did not use, on duplication, things that were bought in two different places or maybe different things that were bought in two different places or two different parts of the organization doing the same thing. They tend not to pay much attention at all to those costs that you incur when you fail to do something you might have done, partly because they never know about it. The out-of-pocket costs are right there in the accounting machine and the opportunity costs we never record, or rarely record.

I have had this point driven home to me recently in some interesting ways in regard to what you do with a library in a university; what you do with a library depends on the person with whom you are talking. If you talk with a librarian, what you do with a library is to put all the books in a central library which grows and grows and grows and where everyone can get what he wants and can get easy access and so on. If you talk with a physicist, what you want in a library is a highly decentralized library with a science library and a science research library; it is all right with him if those humanists want to go over to the other library and read things but naturally they are not going to read anything about physics so why put it over there! But from an organizational point of view, the conspicuous thing is nobody pays any attention to an analysis of what the actual costs are. The only costs that enter into the librarian's calculation of the costs of a library are costs like the clerk to staff one, the cost of space, the costs and so on, and never, at least yet, have I seen anyone in the organization who attempts to calculate the cost of the non-utilization of library books.

Where Supervision Goes Wrong

Now let us talk about what all this might have to do with supervision. Much of our talk about supervision seems to me to be based very heavily on the classic model of an organization. Such a classic model assumed that there is an entrepreneur or a manager, and that through wages, through love, through whatever it is, agreement is sought on the part of subordinates to pursue those objectives. Then they jointly or he singly has discovered the optimal procedures for achieving those objectives.

This assumes basically an organization in which the goals are clear and in which the technology is established and straightforward. In this kind of organization the supervisory problem is fairly simple. You take an individual into the organization, you train him or socialize him or whatever it takes to get him to know what the objectives of the organization are, and what the procedures are. You then direct, control or influence him and you finally evaluate and reward him and that is the kind of work that a supervisor is engaged in. I think that by and large the talk about introducing change in organization proceeds from this same model of an organization. When we talk about the supervisor as a change agent, we are assuming that there is initiative on the part of the supervisor, that his objective is to get those who are supervised to perform appropriately, given the goals and given the technology, or perhaps some new knowledge about the technology. Well, where does this seemingly go wrong?

First this approach assumes that the goal is known. In fact, I think, the major trick in most organizations is to maintain a viable organization without a goal in the usual sense, in a classical sense, a well-defined, consistent objective. I think we have spent a great deal of time saying that the problem is to make the goal concrete, consistent, objective, and that perhaps we ought to take another look and say, "Can you in fact run an organization without such a thing and, if so, how do you do it?" I think the answer is clearly, that you can, because I believe most organizations do. Perhaps you are barking up the wrong tree by putting so much emphasis on trying to improve the unique consistency of operationality of the goal. We ought to turn around and say, "There *is* some way of running an organization."

I have been particularly struck by the need for this when one starts talking about running an illegitimate organization. In that kind of organization, which I think is perhaps closer to an educational institution than a business firm, one of the major problems of running an espionage system, for example, is that you know that the goals are not shared. In fact you do not know what the goals are and somehow in the face of a good deal of ambiguity you have to maintain a system in which you cannot trust anybody, where they cannot trust you, where the goals are changing overnight, and where you want information. Some espionage systems are very effective at this. Or if you look at the organization of narcotic rings. They do some of these kinds of things. Yet if you look at those organizations they are different from the standard bureaucratic organizations. The major narcotic ring in the world for many years, was run entirely by one man, two secretaries, and one loyal assistant. These were the permanent employees. At any point in time there might have been a thousand or more people working for them, but tomorrow there would be a different thousand and none of this thousand had any sense of loyalty. They would have been very happy to execute the boss if they knew who he was and felt it would pay off. So his main problem was to keep a little bit obscure who he was but, more importantly, to make it not profitable to kill him off. Well, there are such organizations, they look more like markets than they look like bureaucracies and perhaps we ought to explore the possibility of supervision in such an organization and perhaps educational institutions are closer to that. In fact, college educational institutions are very close to that.

A second way in which I believe the classical notion of supervision goes wrong is that it probably exaggerates the importance of consistency and coordination among individuals and subgroups and thus incurs heavy costs in lost experimentation, in slack, in independence and so on. Those of us who are in education at its most primitive level, which I take to be in the colleges, are rather reluctant to raise problems of optimal teaching procedures and attempt to regulate the curriculum in a more or less standard way. This may be simply because we know intuitively, or maybe quite consciously, that none of us has any evidence whatsoever that anything that we do makes a bit of difference. If we raise the question of "how can we do it better?" we are going to have to raise the question of "how do we evaluate what we are now doing?" We do not want to do that, so we stick to relatively standard norms of consistency, coordination, standard operating procedures and we tend to resist the notion that the independent entrepreneurs ought to be wandering off in their own direction.

I have made a proposal in at least one educational institution that we adopt a very simple rule for graduation. The proposal is that the requirements for graduation at the University of California at Irvine in social science should be as follows: Each student who is a candidate for graduation must persuade one faculty member that he should get a degree. I proposed this once. My colleagues do not yet think I am serious and in a sense I cannot be because they will not let me be. But what is wrong with the proposal? If I can somehow get the burden of proof on their shoulders, which is the trick in education in general, if I can say before they ask me what evidence there is that this will work. I ask them what evidence is there that their system is better. Then I have them. Because they do not have a scintilla of evidence. But they will not even let me post the alternative. But it is clear what the alternative does.

This proposal would, if we adopted it, get many students through the University of California, without doing any work. And some would not get through who were very smart and did a lot of work, but just happened to choose the wrong faculty member, or could not locate the one who could get them through. And some faculty members would become very popular, and some people would be getting through in one year and some in six years, and there would be great disparity or unfairness and so on. There also would be tremendous experimentation, I believe, in what an education consists of—that is, tremendous as compared with what we are now doing.

What I think is bothering my colleagues about this system is that they are very much concerned about those out-of-pocket costs—the conspicuous costs. For example, what happens when Mary Jones walks in one day to Professor Smith, who is a patsy for good looking blondes and short skirts and says, "I want to graduate." Naturally he says, "All right, let's graduate you," and she graduates. At the same time John Brown, who is a hard-working boy, not very imaginative, but hard-working, straightforward, true blue, square shooter, spends eight years trying to persuade Professor Smelch, who does not think anybody should graduate. Well those are out-of-pocket costs.

A third point at which I think the classical model seems to go wrong is that it ignores the prime problem of many organizations. This is not the problem of deciding what to do, and is not the problem of implementing that decision once you have made it, but it is the problem of discovering alternatives, of generating alternatives. Unless you can design an organization and operate in an organization in which there are some very conscious activities directed toward generating alternatives, then as nearly as I can tell from looking at our studies, you have given away most of the game. For example, when we talk about influencing people, most of the classical models of influence have to do with how you persuade someone to take alternative A rather than alternative B. I guess I am persuaded, at this point of these observations and some experimental studies along the same line, that the primary way in which you can influence someone is by generating a new alternative for him. And the primary way in which an organization is influenced is by getting new alternatives because it is poverty stricken in alternatives. Yet most of the classical models of organizations, most of the classical models of supervision that I know about, just plain ignore this problem or deal with it in a kind of *ad hoc* way.

Related to this is a fourth kind of difficulty, which is that the classical model races into what we have called Gresham's Law of Planning. The real Gresham's Law is that bad money drives out good. Our Gresham's Law is that routine drives out planning, routine drives out thinking. I suppose it is almost a trivial observation to point out that most people in most organizations spend most of the time answering the telephone, or answering the mail, or filling out the forms, or taking the attendance. These are all very useful things at some point or other, but unless you can devise an organization in which you very consciously protect people from the temptations to take the roll, or the temptations to make reports, or the temptations when that box in the classroom belches to belch back at it, we are in trouble. Any time we put demands for such information upon the organization, we are catering to one of our most obscene tastes, which is that most people in most organizations, no matter how much they complain about it, really prefer to take attendance rather than to do interesting things. The only way you can get them to do interesting things is to take away the tablets on which they can write, take away the forms they can fill out, and keep beating them in such a way that they have to think about generating alternatives, doing planning.

If the reader believes what I have said, and I hope he will believe the empirical results, then he may want to quarrel with the derivations. It seems to me there are two prime alternatives. We can change the world or we can change our model. And most of us most of the time would rather change the world for reasons that are a little obscure. And we are doing this to a certain extent. That is, by changing the world, I mean we can create organizations in which there are well-defined objectives, and we can create organizations in which there are people who do precisely what they are supposed to do. I suppose the McNamara revolution in the Department of Defense is of this sort.

Yet we can also experiment with changing the model. A supervisor or an organizer, or an administrator has, I think, an unfortunate bias against anarchy. He tends not to like it. There are some obvious role prescriptions that lead him not to like it. It may well be that in an anarchy we do not need a supervisor or at least we may need a different kind, so that if we are going to change the model we are going to have to change quite basically our notions about supervision. If we are going to build an innovative organization, for example, I suspect that we will shift the focus from *individual supervision* to *organization supervision*. We will worry less about what the individual is doing and worry more about what the organization as a whole is doing.

I suspect that we will use tactics like deliberate ambiguity, and inconsistency of the signals we give, which are quite counter to traditional notions: That the supervisor instead of telling someone exactly what he wants will deliberately confuse this person. That we will protect and try to build in very basic protection from Gresham's Law. That we will encourage competition in alternatives, and that we will attempt at least to build a kind of organization in which people are loosely connected via ill-defined and inconsistent goals in a kind of ambiguous anarchy and to exploit that system rather than attempt to modify that system in a major way toward the kind of system that we think we know how to handle, a system of consistent goals and a well-defined technology.

A Final Note

James Raths

I WOULD like to share with you two concerns about supervision and supervisors that have come to me as I participated in the two sections of the Eleventh Curriculum Research Institute of the Association for Supervision and Curriculum Development. In the eight days that the Institute ran during the past year, I talked with at least 200 supervisors concerning their work, their aspirations, their problems, and their shortcomings. Two difficulties seemed to present themselves over and over again—and in the context of James B. Macdonald's dilemmas elaborated in the first piece of this collection, they are discussed below:

Supervisor's Knowledge of Teaching

The supervisors with whom I spoke seemed very reluctant to admit that they knew more about teaching than their teachers. To suggest that supervisors should know a great deal about teaching seemed to these supervisors tantamount to suggesting a totalitarian system of educational organization. The notion of democratic leadership was raised at this point.

Supervisors are rarely elected, rarely answerable to an electorate for their decisions, and rarely are they appointed for a short term of office. To argue that supervisors can be democratic at all under these circumstances seems to me to use the word in a manner totally different from the way it is normally used. Second, there is a growing amount of research concerning teaching of which supervisors need to become aware—Page, Gage, Hughes, Amidon, Flanders, Macdonald, Allen, Gordon, Waetjen, and Bellack are just a few of the many persons who have reported studies that have important implications for teachers and teaching.

125

While it may be too much to expect recent graduates of teachers colleges to be familiar with these researches, or even to expect the more experienced, busy classroom teachers to spend time reading the recent studies in teaching, clearly the supervisor in his training and on his job must take time out to read and comprehend research reports concerning the teaching-learning process. Clearly, ignorance is no way to start the task of successful supervision—especially as it is hidden behind the cloak of democracy or democratic practices.

Supervisor's Recognition of Means and Ends

So often the concern of supervisors and researchers in supervision is with process. As supervisors, we observe process and rarely take into account the result of the process we have observed. We tend to make judgments about correct processes when, as Macdonald pointed out, we do not have substantial evidence to support the efficacy of one process over another. Is the lecture system wrong in first grade? Wrong for what? It seems to me that it is wrong if it does not meet certain objectives that a rival procedure would adequately meet. Does someone know of any research on the lecture method used at the first grade level? I am not arguing that the ends justify the means. I am arguing that these cannot be separated.

Just as we would resist looking solely at the ends, so we must resist examining only the means. Supervisors, it would seem to me, must be able to differentiate between means and ends—and recognize that no procedure is good in and of itself—but it is good only as it meets certain objectives without harming the attainment of other important goals.

As the two sections of the Curriculum Research Institute progressed, it seemed to me that the distinction between ends and means was not abundantly clear to all of the participants. At the close of some of the sessions, role-playing of supervisory interviews took place. A person playing the role of supervisor would ask a person assuming the role of teacher the following question, "What were your purposes today?" The teacher would respond, "To discuss the observations of our field trip." Very few persons in the audience saw the "teacher's" answer as being non-responsive to the question. Discussing observations is not a purpose, rather it is an activity to attain a purpose.

While this distinction may seem frivolous, it apparently is very important in making decisions about teaching and about supervision. If a teacher is unable to distinguish between an objective and a procedure, then it would seem most difficult for him to plan and carry out his lessons in an exacting and purposeful manner.

In summary, one of the conclusions one must come to as he reads the papers in this booklet is that old cliché: we need more research in supervision. This old cliché is no less true for its tired sound. However, it would seem to me that the evaluation of supervisory practices—such as feedback systems or as having knowledge of teachers' personality patterns—must have as its dependent variable the learnings of children.

Researches that evaluate one process by comparing it with the ratings of another seem fruitless to me. The purpose of supervision is to enhance teaching. One of the central goals of teaching is to attain the goals of the school system. Supervision must be planned and evaluated within this framework if we are to generate reliable knowledge about the supervisory act.